LUMBER SIZES

Always order lumber by its common size, not its actual size.

Common size in inches	Actual size in inches	Common size in inches	Actual size in inches
1 x 2	¾ x 1⅝	2 x 2	1⅝ x 1⅝
1 x 3	¾ x 2⅝	2 x 3	1⅝ x 2⅝
1 x 4	¾ x 3⅝	2 x 4	1⅝ x 3⅝
1 x 6	¾ x 5⅝	2 x 6	1⅝ x 5⅝
1 x 8	¾ x 7½	2 x 8	1⅝ x 7½
1 x 10	¾ x 9½	2 x 10	1⅝ x 9½
1 x 12	¾ x 11½	2 x 12	1⅝ x 11½

NAIL SIZES

Many hardware stores still sell nails by their penny number.

Penny number	Length in inches
2	1
3	1¼
4	1½
5	1¾
6	2
8	2½
10	3
12	3¼

THE FEMININE FIX-IT
HANDBOOK

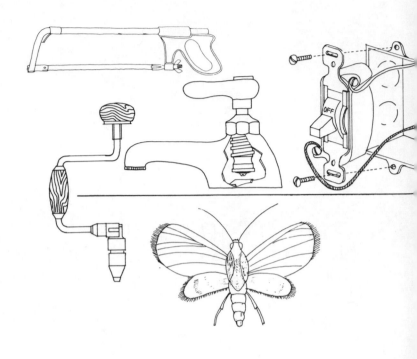

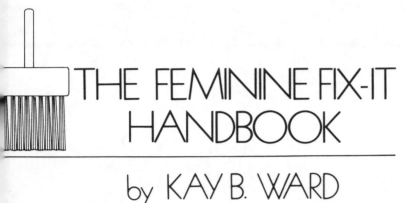

THE FEMININE FIX-IT HANDBOOK

by KAY B. WARD

GROSSET & DUNLAP

A National General Company

Publishers   New York

Contents

Introduction

Yes, this is for you, you helpless feminine bit of fluff. Let's be practical. It would be nice to leave the home repairs to Sam, but for a lot of us, Sam is a very elusive male creature. So for your own convenience and comfort, here is a simple guide to the repair of the little disasters that continually plague mortal woman: the leaky faucet, the peeling paint, the lamp that won't light.

So don your most attractive dungarees and your most alluring sweat shirt and let's cut through the mysteries of the problem and simply "fix it."

1. Your Tools and Their Uses

Surprisingly few tools are needed for basic home repairs. Unless you plan to go into more sophisticated contracting, here are all the tools you should need, with instructions on how to use them. Don't skimp on cost because a good tool is worth the money invested.

Hammer	Pliers
Saw	Adjustable wrench
Brace and bit (drill)	Staple gun
Screwdriver	Threaded awl

Forgive me if I seem to oversimplify. It is *not* a reflection on your intellect but on my assumption that you have never really confronted a hammer and saw.

HAMMER

In theory, there are only two things you should legitimately do with a hammer: drive a nail or pull out a nail. To drive a nail, hold the nail between your thumb and index finger. With the other hand, hold the hammer near

1

the end of the handle. Gently tap the nail until it stands up by itself.

Now let go of the nail and, swinging harder, strike the head of the nail squarely so it will not bend. Don't despair if you're clumsy at this at first. With a little practice you'll feel quite confident.

To draw out a nail, use the claw end of the hammer. If the nail head is flush against the surface, pry it up a bit with your screwdriver. If it's one of those funny nails with hardly any head and you can't draw it out, try tapping it farther in with a bigger, blunted nail and pulling it through the opposite side with pliers. Or, if there is no opposite side to pull it through, just tap it in farther (countersink it) and fill the hole with wood putty or plastic wood.

Here is a hint for neatly drawing out a nail. Place a small block of wood against the hammer head to use as a wedge so that the nail comes out straighter. You'll find you leave a much smaller hole and will have used a lot less effort.

SAW

You will find two saws useful: the crosscut saw for cutting wood or plasterboard and the hacksaw for metal.

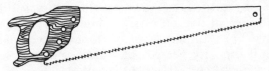

For an all-purpose wood saw, I recommend the one pictured here. It will suit your general needs. An important rule to remember is: let the saw do most of the work. Never force the saw or put pressure on it. If you have a good saw it will do the work while you just guide it and gently urge it forward.

Hold the wood firmly. Start at your mark with short strokes to get a bite so that the saw will not jump. Once you get going, use long, slow strokes. Remember, your saw is twenty-four inches long. No need to use only eight inches worth.

You may run into some of the following problems at first:

1. You've started out fine but unconsciously you have angled your saw blade and the saw comes to a screeching, protesting halt. Your best solution is to start over.

2. You're sawing a length of wood and suddenly all sorts of ghastly screaming noises come from the reluctant saw. Perhaps the saw is being pinched by the wood already cut. Lean down on the cut material as indicated in the drawing.

3. You're forcing your saw along and suddenly it will not cut one bit farther. The blade was probably bowed in a warped shape because you were not holding it properly. Start over, holding the saw squarely. Here is the correct way of handling it.

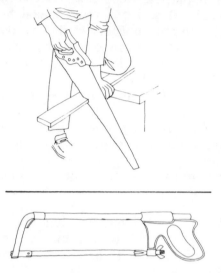

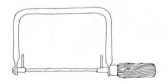

The hacksaw, pictured above, is a handy tool for cutting off nails, heavy wire, cable or small pieces of metal. I would not suggest attempting to make a convertible of your sedan with this tool, but it is invaluable on smaller jobs. Do not confuse this tool with the coping saw (below), which is used to cut curves and other fancy shapes in thin wood or plastic.

BRACE AND BIT

Translated, this means the drill (bit) and the holder for the drill (brace). I prefer the type of hand drill illustrated here only because you can lean more weight into it and as a result have better control over it. To use

it, first determine the size of the hole to be drilled. Select a bit of the corresponding size and insert the shaft part of the bit into the jaws of the bit holder (chuck) on the brace. These jaws may be opened and closed by twisting the screw mechanism on the brace directly above the jaws. Close the jaws so that they clamp securely on the shaft of the bit.

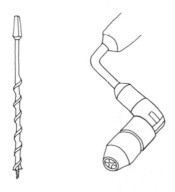

Be sure that the work to be drilled is firmly secured, and then proceed as shown in this illustration.

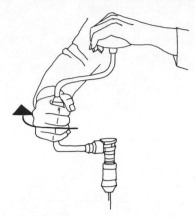

If you plan to do many home repairs, consider investing in an electric drill. If you can hold it steady and drill smoothly without forcing it, it's much easier to handle and less tiring to use than any manual drill. Directions on how to change bits come with the tool.

SCREWDRIVER

I expect that for now you need only concern yourself with the standard-shaped screwdriver. The sizes which fit the most widely used screws have a blade about $\frac{3}{16}$ inch wide. The little chunky fellow shown is handy for awkward places and fits nicely in the palm of your hand.

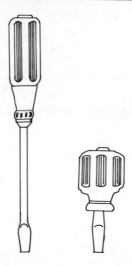

Buy the driver that feels good in your hand, with a handle that's not so smooth that your palm slips on it yet not so lumpy that it gives you blisters. Again, don't buy an inexpensive one. A good tool won't chip or become battered and chewed.

A screwdriver was designed only for driving or removing screws. But (don't tell your purist brother-in-law this) it can also be used for opening paint cans, prying up nail heads and innumerable other tasks.

PLIERS

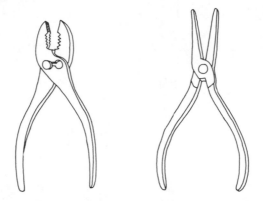

These are the only two types of pliers necessary for the home repairwoman. The mechanic's pliers have a peculiar double joint which allows them to act normally or, in the double-joint position, open wider for larger items. These versatile jaws will also accept and cut wire if you place it well back within the jaws.

The long nose pliers are not exceptionally strong but they can wriggle into small, awkward places. They are invaluable in electrical work for wrapping wire around a terminal and are also handy for holding a small nut while a bolt is being screwed onto it.

ADJUSTABLE WRENCH
(crescent or open end wrench)

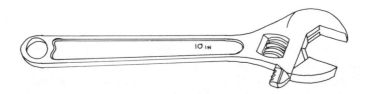

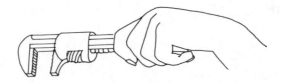

Both the wrenches pictured do essentially the same job, which is to remove a nut from a bolt or a collar from threading. You will see, as we proceed, how many uses each of these wrenches has.

If you plan to run a one-wrench shop, get an adjustable wrench large enough for your basic needs. I would suggest one that opens to its widest at 2¾ to 3 inches.

THREADED AWL

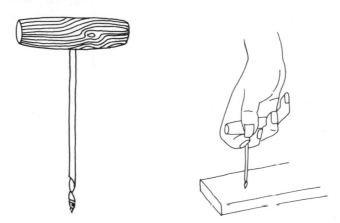

High on my list of absolutes is the threaded awl. This useful tool is most handy for starting holes for small screws, cup hooks, etc. You should never try to put a screw into wood or other material without first making a pilot or starter hole. The larger the screw, the larger the pilot hole. For larger holes you will need to use a drill but for small jobs this tool is a positive jewel.

STAPLE GUN

This is another invaluable tool. It's perfect for small upholstery jobs, putting new screening onto a screen frame, remounting the backing on a picture frame and yet-unthought-of tasks. You will often find it a fine substitute for a hammer and tacks.

This should make a pretty complete home kit for you. Any tools that are needed for specific jobs, such as paint brushes, putty knives, etc., will be mentioned in future chapters.

HARDWARE

Nails.   Illustrated here are some of the basic nails with which you may come in contact.

1. Common nail. This rough-and-ready nail comes in a variety of lengths. It is most often used for general construction work.

2. Finishing nail. The advantage of this nail for finished work is that it may be countersunk (see Glossary) and the hole filled with putty or filler. This makes it almost impossible to see the nail spot.

3. Brad. This is a small, thin finishing nail which is used for small jobs. It is very often used as an "insurance" fastener when a wooden object is to be glued.

4. Masonry or cut nail. This nail can penetrate brick, concrete or concrete block. It can be used to hang a picture on this type of wall, but be forewarned that it takes perseverance.

5. Upholsterers nail. Bet you can't guess what this one's for.

6. Carpet tack. Nor this one either.

Never but never try to nail a screw into an object. Chances are you'll do nothing but split or shred the wood. As previously described in the Threaded Awl section, make a pilot hole before you insert the screw.

Screws.   Illustrated here are some of the more common screws.

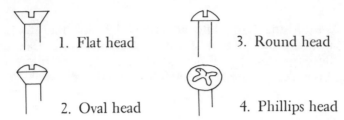

1. Flat head   3. Round head

2. Oval head   4. Phillips head

Look around your home. You will see many of these screws and will get an idea of their many, varied uses. Please note that if you have any phillips head screws, you will need to buy a phillips head screwdriver. Trying to use a standard screwdriver will ruin both the screw and your screwdriver.

Bolts.   The function of the particular bolts illustrated here will be described in the next chapter.

1. Molly bolt

2. Expansion bolt and plug

3. Toggle bolt

The standard bolt to which a nut is threaded has a wide variety of uses. You will find many around your home.

Hooks.   Here is an assortment of hooks which are handy for household needs.

1. L-screw

2. Screw eye

3. Cup hook

4. Hitch ring

For more specialized equipment my suggestion is to go to the hardware store, make friends with the salespeople and investigate the hardware available. There's a piece for almost every need.

2. Hang It on the Wall

In order to explain how to hang your favorite cabinet, shelf or ancestor's portrait I will begin with a short explanation of wall construction.

There are basically two types of wall: the solid wall and the hollow wall. Below are cut-away views of each.

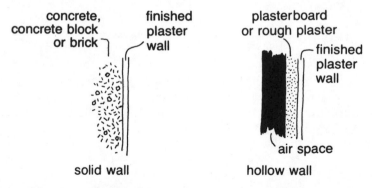

Outside walls or walls between apartments are *usually* solid walls, made of concrete, concrete block or brick. Inside walls or walls separating rooms in your apartment or house are *usually* hollow, made of plaster or plasterboard. Unfortunately, without X-ray equipment or see-through eyes there is no foolproof way of determining which is solid and which is hollow. I can only suggest that you tap the wall to find if it sounds hollow or solid, or drill into a hidden area of the wall with your brace and bit and note how it feels. If it's solid, you'll meet resistance about one-fourth to one-half inch into the wall. That means two things: 1. Life will now be more difficult and 2. You need a tool called a star, or masonry, drill. If the wall is hollow, after drilling for about an inch the drill will poke into the air space and will drill no more.

THE SOLID WALL

Suppose you wish to hang a shelf on a particular wall. The wall looks friendly enough: nice smooth plaster with a pleasant pastel tint of paint on top. But under this pleasing veneer lurks a wall of solid concrete.

Your shelf looks like this, and your problem is, how do you attach the brackets to the wall?

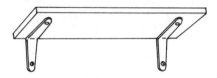

The basic theory is to drill a hole into the wall, insert a plug into the hole and screw the screw into the plug. This action will expand the plug and thus firmly hold the plug and screw in the wall.

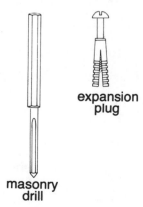

expansion
plug

masonry
drill

You'll need some anchors. I've found that ¼-inch lead plugs with corklike covers work nicely for most household jobs. Also buy the screws to fit. They usually are sold together.

Buy a ¼-inch star, or masonry, drill. This is not expensive and will drill into any type of masonry (concrete, concrete block, etc.). If you have an electric drill there is a special masonry bit which will fit it.

Proceed as follows, step by step.

1. Make pencil marks on the wall where you want your screws to go. On each pencil mark make a small starter hole with your threaded awl. Hold your star drill against the starter hole and, keeping the drill perpendicular to the wall, give it a couple of raps with your hammer. Then rotate the drill to prevent its jamming. Establish a rhythm: tap, tap, rotate; tap, tap, rotate. This is slow work but gradually a hole will be drilled. (An electric drill with a masonry bit will be easier and quicker.) Make sure

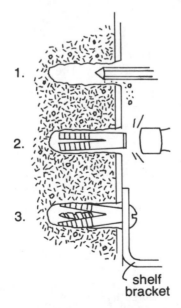

shelf
bracket

that the drilled hole is slightly deeper than the length of the screw. *Close your eyes* and blow out any excess dust from the hole.

2. With your hammer, gently tap the plug into the newly drilled hole. Drill *all* the necessary holes and insert *all* the plugs before proceeding with Step 3.

3. Hold the shelf bracket against the wall, matching the bracket's screw holes with the holes of the plugs. Insert each screw, turning it a couple of times by hand. Take your screwdriver and drive the screw in as far as you can (the screw head should of course be larger than the hole in the bracket). When the screw is driven into the lead plug, the plug expands in its hole, pressing against the sides of the hole, thus making a firm hold in the wall.

Anything you want to hang on a solid wall may be done in this manner: your electric toothbrush holder, your salt box or your great-uncle's clock and, of course, the drapery rods.

THE HOLLOW WALL

Earlier in this chapter you saw a diagram of a hollow wall. The way to mount a shelf on this type of wall is to drill a hole into the wall and then insert a unit which will grip the back side of the wall as well as the front.

1. Buy universal "molly" anchors. The ¼-inch size

should do this job. Insert your ¼-inch bit into the brace (or the ¼-inch bit into the electric drill). Make pencil marks on the wall where you want the screw holes of the bracket to appear. On each pencil mark make a small starter hole with your threaded awl. Now hold the ¼-inch bit against the starter hole and drill into the wall. You can usually feel when your drill bites into the solid matter and later when it becomes free in the air space behind.

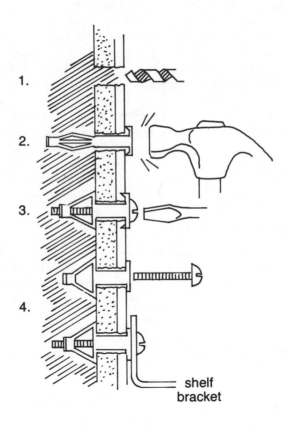

shelf
bracket

2. Remove the screw from the molly bolt and insert the shield into the hole. With your hammer tap it gently until its head is flush against the wall. You will note that at the head of the shield there is a lip with two or three tiny, sharp points. These points will bite into the plaster as you gently tap the shield into the hole. This will keep the unit from twisting around uselessly as you continue.

3. Now insert the screw into the shield, driving it with your screwdriver as deeply as it will go. What you cannot see happening is pictured in the diagram. As you drive in the screw, the portion of the shield which is in the air space bends and is drawn tight against the back side of the wall. Drill all necessary holes, insert and bend up tight all shields before proceeding with Step 4.

4. Again, remove the screws. Place the bracket against the molly-bolt shields, matching the holes. Insert each screw and draw it up tight.

As stated in the Solid Wall section, anything heavy (within reason) may be mounted on the wall in this manner.

If you plan to hang a light pair of curtains, the screws or nails included with the curtain rod will usually be sufficient to hold the light-weight curtains. But drive these nails and screws gently as plaster walls chip, crumble and crack easily.

DOORS

The jacknut, a handy device that works in theory like the molly bolt, is used on thin material such as the plywood of a flush door (a hollow door; flat, without panels) or a wood-paneled wall.

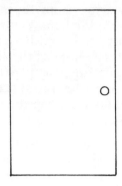

As an example, you can hang a mirror on the back of a hollow door.

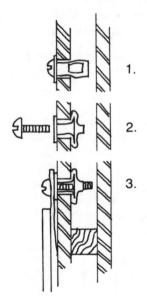

1. Drill the holes through *only* the plywood thickness on the side of the door on which you plan to hang the mirror.

2. Gently tap the jacknut shields into the holes. Insert the screws and expand the shields as shown above.

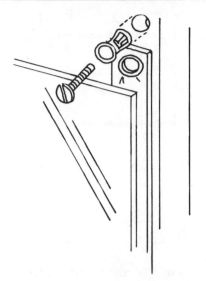

3. Remove the screws and align the hardware on the mirror with the jacknut shields. Again insert the screws and tighten them.

To hang the mirror on a panel door (a door with a thick wood frame and a thin center panel of wood),

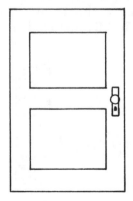

attach a wood strip with screws to the thick framing, keeping the holes aligned. Then, with a slightly heavier screw, screw each end of the wood strip to the door as shown here.

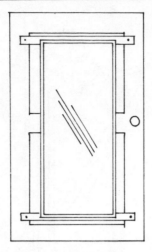

You can also use a T-nut to attach this mirror to the thin part of a paneled door. This works nicely but it does leave a rather unsightly metal fixture showing on the back of the door. If this is the solution for you,

1. Drill through the thin panel of the door.

2. On the opposite side from which the mirror is to be hung, tap in the T-nuts. You will notice that their little teeth will grip to hold the nuts in place.

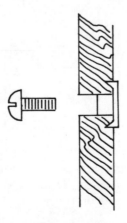

3. From the mirror side, align the hardware on the mirror with the T-nut and insert and tighten the screws.

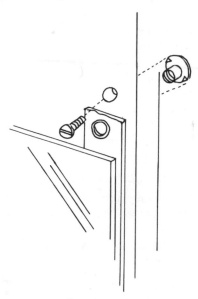

PICTURE HANGING

Many types of fixtures for hanging pictures are sold commercially. Just follow the directions on these packets. They will usually tell you the weight which a particular size fixture will sustain.

For very lightweight items and small, light pictures, the self-stick hangers are sufficient.

For items up to about thirty-five pounds the angled hanger and nail is successful.

For your huge ancestor, that large oil landscape or your great-uncle's clock, the heavy-duty fasteners like those used for the shelf in the beginning of this chapter will be necessary.

If your frame has no hook or wire on the back of it for hanging, do the following:

1. Go to your hardware store and ask for screw eyes (see picture in Chapter 1) and picture wire. This wire is made of six or eight fine wires woven together like rope. The screw eyes come in various sizes. Just tell the clerk the approximate weight of the item to be hung.

2. With the threaded awl make two pilot holes in the correct positions on the back of the frame. Insert the screw eyes and turn them by hand as far as they will go. All but the hardest wood frames will accept the screw eyes easily. Turn them somewhat tighter with pliers.

3. Attach the wire with about the amount of tension shown in this illustration. (If it is too loose, the wire will show from behind the picture. Too tight and the picture will slide and become crooked.)

A rule to keep in mind is that the higher the screw eyes are positioned on the frame, the flatter the picture will hang on the wall. The lower the screw eyes are positioned, the more the picture will tilt away from the wall.

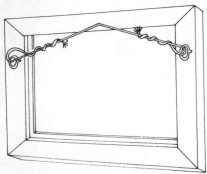

To hang a small picture flush against the wall the following fixtures can be used instead of picture wire. They are simple to attach and lie flat against the frame.

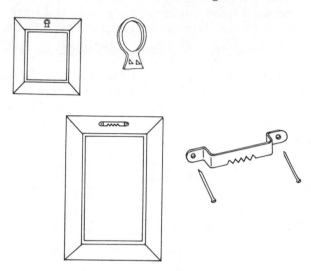

Many decorative items in brass, stainless steel, ornate chains and cords are now sold. Here are a couple of examples to show how they can be handled.

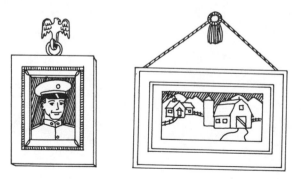

Use your imagination and look at the varied and interesting items on the market today. Look at interior decorating and home magazines for suggestions on styles, positions and groupings.

HANGING CUP HOOKS
AND COAT HOOKS

Here is where your threaded awl earns its real keep.

Most hooks like the ones for hanging cups or sweaters and coats are small and can be screwed in by hand or with the help of pliers to turn the hook. Make a pilot hole with the threaded awl and just screw in the hook. Investigate your hardware store and five and ten cent store and see what is available. There is also hardware for hanging mops, brooms, ironing boards, towels. So look around and follow the directions on the packaging.

WALL UNITS
AND SPACE SAVERS

Many companies manufacture completely finished shelves, cabinets, magazine racks and drawers which you can put together in units and hang on the wall to suit your particular needs.

For instance, you can install an entertainment unit on a living-room wall.

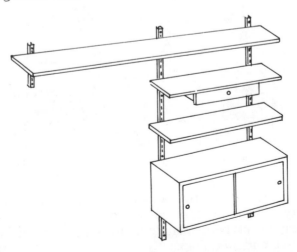

Or a work area in the kitchen.

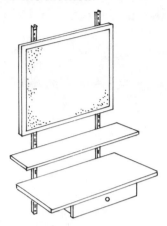

Or an office.

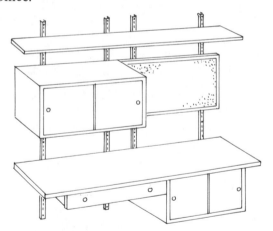

You'll find these units will work in every room in the house. You can also build your own units by finishing raw cabinets or shelving (see Chapter 10) and purchasing the standards separately. If you are making shelves, you can have the shelving precut to your specifications at a lumberyard.

Here's how to hang a wall unit.

1. Following the directions given earlier in the chapter, install the standards on the wall.

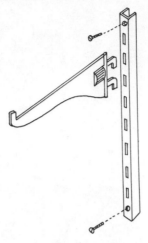

If your wall is hollow, you *must* attach the standards to the studs (the structural two-by-fours behind the plaster). Otherwise your shelf is likely to end up on the floor. Use wood screws and see Chapter 9, page 128, for directions on finding the studs.

2. Now measure the width of your shelf and find the appropriate shelf bracket. Place it into the slots of the standard and press downward so that the feet on the bracket lock into the standard slot.

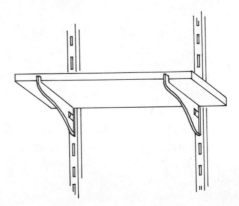

3. You will see a small thumb screw at the base of the bracket. Tighten this to keep the bracket from swinging left or right.

4. Place the finished shelf on the two brackets. I'd advise you to test out your shelf with something replaceable to be sure it's sturdy. You don't want to install your new stereo or rearrange all your books, only to discover that upon installation you forgot to do something vital!

Using the same theory of standard and bracket, you can make room dividers using floor-to-ceiling expandable standard poles. For instance, you can separate a dining area from your living room.

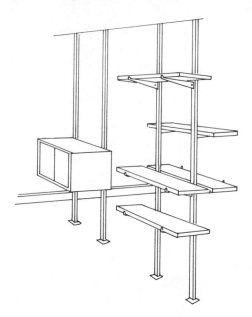

Whether your decor is modern, Mediterranean or Early American, you can buy or make an attractive, harmonious wall unit. Look at your lumberyard, decorator magazines and your friends' homes. You'll soon find yourself coming up with your own ideas for your walls.

3. Redecorating
With Paint

Painting a room yourself is a rewarding accomplishment and is especially rewarding to your pocketbook.

It sounds easy . . . buy some paint and a brush and apply the paint to the wall with the brush. But don't be fooled. It's hard physical work but not work beyond your ability.

I know you're anxious to see that fresh, sparkling, new paint on the wall but don't be hasty. You must do certain preliminaries if the actual painting is not to be a waste of time. Then you will have a job you're really proud of.

The first step is to buy all the materials you will need.

BUYING YOUR EQUIPMENT

Brushes. As in buying tools, don't skimp on cost. A good paint brush is worth the money paid. If you plan to use a roller (which I would advise for a broad expanse of ceiling and wall) you will also need two basic brushes. One is a 2½- to 3-inch flat brush for painting doors, trim and the corners of the room which the roller doesn't quite reach. The other is an angled sash brush of 1½- to 2-inch width for cutting cleanly into windows and frames.

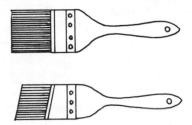

If your wall is textured or rough and a deep-pile roller won't cover the texture properly, you will need a larger brush. I would advise a 4-inch flat brush. This will cover a fairly large area and at the same time is not too cumbersome to handle (a large brush full of paint is surprisingly heavy).

Are there any pipes to be painted? Then it's advisable to purchase a round or oval brush for convenience.

Rollers and trays.   You can purchase rollers with many different types of roller cover. The following are the most popular:

1. Short-nap mohair covers used for glossy or semi-gloss enamels.

2. Medium-length nap for most walls and ceilings. This is the one you will probably want.

3. Deep-pile rollers for rough surfaces (concrete, stucco or roughly decorated plaster).

I would advise buying an 8-inch-long roller and cover.

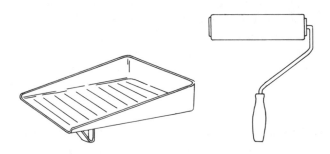

You may want to buy an extra roller cover just for convenience. If you plan to reuse them, buy plastic-cored roller covers, as the cardboard covers will fall apart when you wash them out. Make sure that when the roller cover is on the roller it turns easily and works smoothly, and that it is designed to be taken apart easily. Remember that any complicated screw-ons or wing nuts can become crusted with paint and nearly impossible to remove for cleaning. Usually an aluminum paint tray comes with the roller as a set. If that is not the case make sure you buy a tray.

Tools to prepare the wall.   To fill holes and cracks in the wall you will need the following materials:

> 1. A prepared spackle compound to use for filling small holes and cracks. This is a premixed, plaster-like substance which comes in a can.

> 2. A putty knife or broad knife to smooth out the spackled or plaster-filled hole so it's flush with the wall.
>
> 3. Patching plaster which comes in a powder form and must be mixed with water (follow directions on the bag). Use this plaster for larger cracks and holes. If you plan to do a very large area, say one foot by one foot, don't expect perfect results. Plastering takes a good deal of experience, and we are amateurs.

Drop cloths.   A salute to plastic! For under a dollar you can buy a 9- by 12-foot plastic cloth for covering furniture and floors. It's worth buying a couple. You might also save some newspapers to spread around to avoid a trail of paint footprints.

Sticks, pails, rags, sundries. If you don't have a good supply of clean mixing sticks from the backyard, you can buy them at the paint store for very little money. You can also buy inexpensive cardboard pails for mixing the paint. A medium-fine carbon sandpaper will come in handy for smoothing newly plastered walls. Three or four sheets should do.

You can never have too many rags. Always keep one handy as you work, tucked in a waistband or pocket. An immediate swipe with a rag at a misplaced blob of paint can save a lot of scrubbing two hours later.

Paint. I strongly advise using one of the water-soluble paints. They cover easily and well, they dry quickly, the odor is not strong and doesn't linger and, most important, washing up is done with water. These latex paints come in both semigloss (slightly shiny) and flat (no shine at all).

For a bedroom, living or dining room you will most likely want flat latex for the walls and ceilings and semigloss for the trim (windows, sashes, doors and door frames).

In a kitchen or bath I would suggest using semigloss on the walls as it can be washed more easily than flat paint.

Your paint dealer will advise you on the amount to buy if you tell him the dimensions of your room. Read the directions on the paint can and follow them.

BEFORE YOU PAINT

Now that all the equipment is assembled, you are ready to prepare the walls for painting.

1. Remove as many items as possible from the room. If this can't be done pile as much as possible in the center of the room and cover this with one or two plastic drop cloths.

2. Clean the walls, ceilings and woodwork as paint will cover properly only on clean surfaces. Vacuuming or dusting is usually all that's necessary. However, kitchen walls and ceilings in areas where grease might have splattered should be scrubbed with a detergent.

3. If any paint is peeling, attack it with the flat edge of your broad knife or with a wire brush. Remove as much as possible. If any areas are bubbling with loose plaster or peeling wallpaper, scrape it away with your broad knife. Get rid of it now or it may fall in a heap after you've painted over it.

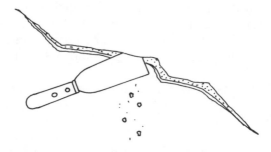

4. Scrape all cracks and holes free of chipped paint and loose plaster. Then undercut the crack (scrape away wider on the inside of the crack than at the surface) to insure a good bond. A corner of your putty knife scraped along the crack and around the rim of the hole should take care of this.

Remove the prepared spackle from the can with your putty knife and pack it into the crack or hole. Build it up slightly thicker or higher than the surface of the wall. Then take your putty knife or broad knife and smooth it along the wall to get rid of the excess spackle. A few hours later, when the

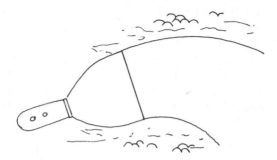

spackle has thoroughly dried, sand it smooth with the medium-fine sandpaper.

5. If there are any holes bigger than your thumb or cracks as wide as that same thumb, you will need patching plaster. Do not use spackle for these larger jobs as it will shrink and crack while drying. Mix the plaster as directed on the package. After undercutting and dusting out the crack to remove loose particles, wet the crack with clear water. Pack a small layer of mixed plaster into the crack, filling it about half full. Allow this to harden before you apply the next layer (plaster dries enough in about twenty minutes). The second layer should almost fill the crack. After this has dried, wet the surface again with clear water and add more plaster to bring the level up to the wall's surface. Smooth it as evenly as possible with the broad knife. When this has thoroughly dried, use the medium-fine sandpaper to rub the area smooth. Wipe the area to remove any plaster dust. Allow the area to dry for twenty-four hours.

6. Now, using a special paint primer and sealer, paint the spackled or newly plastered areas with the 2½-inch flat brush. If this isn't done patchy spots may show in these areas.

7. Before things get out of control, get to work with a dustpan and broom. Get rid of plaster dust, chips and flakes.

8. After turning off the electricity (see Chapter 6), go around the room and with your screwdriver, take out the screws and remove all switch plates. These are the neat-looking covers that hide the innards of the light switches. Removing them makes the painting a bit easier and tidier. You could drop the ceiling light fixtures, but rather than go into the complexities of doing this I'll advise leaving them and using care when you paint around them. Now you're ready to paint!

PAINTING, STEP BY STEP

The ceiling and walls

1. Set the paint can on some old newspapers. Open the lid with a screwdriver, prying it off gradually from place to place all around the can. If you concentrate on prying it only on one side, chances are you'll get the lid off all out of shape so that it can no longer be put back.

2. Stir the paint with a clean mixing stick until it is of an equal consistency from the bottom of the can to the top. If it doesn't mix to your satisfaction (an older can of paint may not) pour some into a cardboard pail, mix the paint in the can, pour back from the pail, mix, pour into the pail, etc. After the paint is mixed, it might be easier to pour about one-third of the paint into the cardboard pail and work from this instead of contending with the big gallon of paint.

3. Always begin with the ceiling. These days it is not necessary to ask for a special ceiling paint. The popular brands usually come all in one. Start with the 2½- or 3½-inch flat brush and paint all around the room where the ceiling meets the wall. Unfortunately the roller won't sneak into these corners. Be

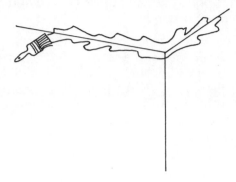

ncat, please. No blobs or bare spots. Cover the area with even strokes and be careful that you don't splatter down the wall. Wipe any splatters up as you go along or they'll dry in hard knobs. Don't dip your brush too deeply into the paint. If you don't keep the paint well below the metal bristle holder you will find it dripping down your arm and off your elbow.

4. Once the corners are done you're ready for the roller. You'll find this the quickest part of the job. Pour some paint into the roller tray (about 1½ to 2 inches in the deep end). You should be able to press out the excess paint in the shallow end of the tray. Role the roller slowly down the sloping tray to the deep end and then back up to the shallow end. This should distribute the paint evenly in the roller. Place the roller against the ceiling and roll the first stroke away from you. Do not press hard. Roll in long back-and-forth strokes, smoothing out your initial stroke. Try to roll in one back-and-forth direction. Reload the roller and continue. Don't be concerned if the results look uneven as you proceed. Latex paint dries in patches but it should be flat and even in about an hour.

You can use a long-handled extension with the roller for the ceiling. However I feel that I have more control without it. On a good, sturdy stepladder close to the work I can wipe up as needed and see missed spots more readily.

5. Now you're ready to start the walls. Use your brush again to paint the corners where wall meets wall. If the walls are to be a different color than the ceiling, brush with the paint brush neatly along the top of the wall, meeting the ceiling color. This is a chore the roller won't do well and it may be painstaking. When this is done, paint the walls with the roller, using the same method as for the ceiling.

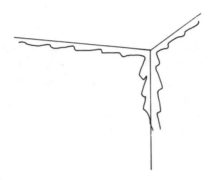

6. Things should be shaping up nicely now and you have every right to be proud of yourself. Keep up the good work and go on to the trim.

Doors, windows and trim

1. As mentioned earlier, a semigloss paint on woodwork is easier to keep clean and wash than the flat paint. Dip the brush (bristles only) into the paint. Apply the paint and feather it out smoothly and lightly with long strokes in one direction. Do all the baseboards, window and door frames and windowsills with this paint.

2. Since a door is a flat area upon which small flaws are magnified, it should be painted carefully. For a clean job, follow this lettered sequence. Avoid dribbles (widows) and spread the paint on evenly.

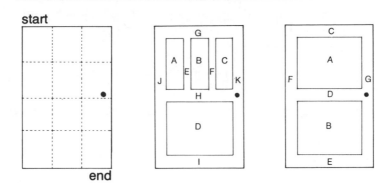

3. To paint a window, use the sash brush and a laundry shirt cardboard (or something similar) to "cut in" (paint) the window frames around the glass. Hold the cardboard against the window glass to shield it from the paint.

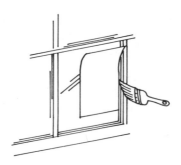

If the paint does get on the glass, it is easier to let it dry and scrape it the next day with a single-edged razor blade. Don't let paint sit for a week or more on the window glass or you'll have a bad time trying to scrape it off. It sets very well on glass.

4. How do you get at all the parts of a window without discovering three days later that you've missed a section? A casement window doesn't present too much trouble. Just follow the lettered sequence indicated. But take a good look at the double-hung one! I suggest you follow the order noted

below by first raising the lower sash as high as it will go and lowering the upper sash about halfway. Paint these areas in sequence.

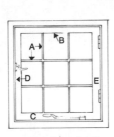

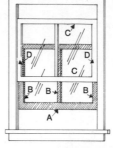

casement window   double hung window

Then lower the bottom sash to its normal position and raise the top sash until it's about two inches clear of the top. Paint these areas. Last, paint the edges of the sashes and the trim, ending with the sill. Remember! Leave the window open a bit at the top and bottom to prevent its sticking as the paint dries.

5. Chances are the latex paint will have covered everything in one coat. But if you are painting over a dark color you will probably need a second coat. This can be done in a matter of hours as the latex paint dries so quickly.

Washing up isn't exactly a joy but if you have ever used oil paint you will appreciate the simplicity of this operation with water-soluble paints. Everything goes in the bathtub or sink with water—brushes, rollers, empty paint tray, etc. Squeeze and rinse the roller cover under running water until the water appears clear. Wash your good brushes thoroughly and dry them carefully. They can give a lot of service if treated kindly.

Built-in cabinets and shelves

1. The most convenient way to paint cabinets,

whether they be in the kitchen, bedroom or play-room, is to remove the doors. Painting these doors flat rather than upright avoids dribbling and blob-bing. Take down the doors by removing the screws which attach the hinges to the doors.

2. After you have removed the doors, unscrew the door handles or knobs. Sand the doors to a smooth finish. Paint kitchen cabinet doors with glossy, quick-drying enamel because the grease and soot which are the distress of any kitchen cleaning wash off easily. For other doors use a semigloss enamel. (You may wish to use an aerosol spray. You will probably use quite a lot of paint this way but the surface will be smooth. Remember! Work with good ventilation!)

3. Apply the first coat. Don't dip the brush into the paint too deeply. Dip only about one half the length of the bristles to avoid splashes and mess. Check the underside to be sure no drips show. After the doors have dried, sand them with a very fine sandpaper. Clean up the sanding dust.

4. Apply the second coat, again checking the under-side for drips. Turn the doors over and paint the op-posite side. When all doors are completely painted, set them aside and let them dry flat.

5. Now go back to the cabinets themselves and paint them inside and out. Let them dry, sand them, dust out the sandings and give them a final coat. To apply the final coat of enamel, cover the item by stroking paint on in one direction and gentling it out in the opposite direction.

Stand back and admire what you have done. You're marvelous!

Don't be timid about asking your local paint dealer questions. He should be happy to answer them. He can give you advice about unusual paints and extra tips for doing floors, ceilings and special walls.

4. Redecorating With Wallpaper

Applying paper can be as satisfying as putting a fresh coat of paint on the walls. Do not let the idea of papering frighten you. Just follow the directions step by step and keep your cool.

YOUR EQUIPMENT

Work table.   You'll need somewhere to work flat, to measure the paper, cut it properly and apply the paste as needed. If you have a picnic table or old worktable, fine. If not, you can rig up something with sawhorses or chairs and an old door or boards. Some wallpaper stores lease tables to customers.

Wallpaper kit.   You can find this handy kit in most stores which carry wallpaper. It contains a brush for applying paste, a brush for smoothing the paper, a seam roller and a cutting knife. The kit usually includes a set of instructions. You can also purchase all these items separately.

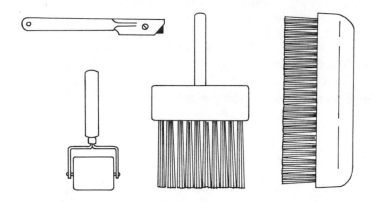

Plumb line. This is a long string with a small weight on the end. It is used to make squared vertical lines on the wall.

Pail. You will need this to mix the paste. A plastic pail would be best but a cardboard one may purchased inexpensively at the wallpaper store.

Scissors, single-edged razor blades, straight edge and ruler. These are necessary for measuring, cutting and and trimming the paper.

Bowl and sponge. Keep a bowl of clear water and a sponge handy to clean up as you go along.

Paste. Your dealer should recommend the best type of paste for the paper you choose.

Paper. Modern wallpapers are much stronger than you might imagine. They are less likely to tear when wet and less like to stain when accidents occur. I strongly advise that you buy paper with the selvages (waste paper along the sides) pretrimmed. There are also a great many patterns available with adhesive on the back, waiting to be moistened. If you are using paper which must have paste applied, buy adhesive paste which does not stain.

Completely washable—in fact, scrubbable—vinyl materials are available that can be used very successfully in kitchens and bathrooms. However, special adhesive and extra care will probably be needed with them. Follow the manufacturer's suggestions and instructions. Take special care if you use a flocked paper as it can stain fairly easily.

HOW TO PAPER

1. After all the above equipment has been gathered, follow the directions in Chapter 3 if the walls to be papered require patching. Turning off the electricity, remove all light-switch plates and wall-plug plates with your screwdriver.

2. If you are planning to paper over a previously painted or newly plastered wall, it will be necessary to give the wall a coat of wall size (a glue solution sold in powder form and mixed with water). Wipe this on with a sponge. Be sure, if the wall was painted, that all loose paint has been scraped off.

You can apply new wallpaper directly over old paper if the old paper is still adhering tightly to the wall. Tear away all loose edges and scrape the rough, torn edge on the wall with a knife or use sandpaper so that that paper will be "feathered" where it meets the wall. (Otherwise when you apply the new paper an unsightly ridge will appear at that point.)

3. As floors and ceilings are rarely straight and square it is not advisable to precut exactly sized lengths of wallpaper. When you measure a length of paper from the roll, always allow about three inches extra at the top and the bottom of the cut strip. This excess, which will overlap onto the ceiling at the top and the baseboard at the bottom, should be trimmed off later with a single-edged razor blade.

4. Now you are ready for the adhesive operation. Choose the most insignificant corner of the room on which to start, only because as you go around the room you will find that the last strip, which will fall next to the first strip, may not exactly match the first strip. This is because of the variation in the square of the room.

Coat the string of the plumb line with chalk. Hold it at the ceiling and against the wall at the same distance from the corner of the room as the wallpaper is wide (approximately three feet). When

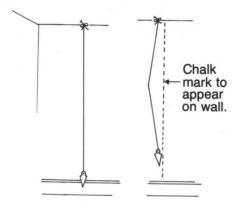

Chalk mark to appear on wall.

the plumb line has stopped swinging (this will be gravity's exact vertical) slap the string lightly like a bow string against the wall. This will make an exact vertical chalk line against the wall. You will use this line as your square.

5. Lay a strip of paper, design down, on the long table (the paste will be applied on the back). As

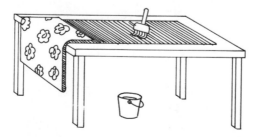

the strip will probably be longer than the table, apply paste with the paste brush to slightly more than half the length of the paper. Then fold (don't crease) this pasted portion against itself so the pattern side is out. Slide this folded section to the end of the table so that you can paste the unfolded portion. Then fold (don't crease) it against itself as you did with the first portion. The adhesive dries uncomfortably fast so don't go away at this point.

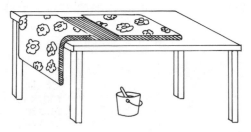

6. Apply the first strip so that it goes slightly (about one to two inches) around the corner of the wall.

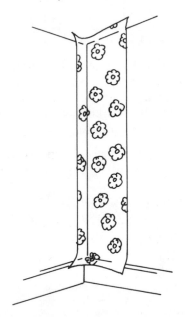

Do not use the corner as your vertical. Use the plumb-line chalk mark.

Place each strip next to the previous strip with space between. Then when it is positioned up and down slide it over to match and butt against the previous strip. Take your time. If you position a strip wrong, pull it off immediately and put it on again. Work quickly but not hastily.

7. After you have hung two or three strips, roll over the seams with the seam roller. If you are using an embossed or textured material, pat the seams firmly with a sponge instead, as the roller would press out the texture or embossing.

If excess paste gets on your paper or comes out from the seams, wipe it away quickly with a damp sponge. Wipe down each piece with a sponge as it is hung to remove any paste or fingerprints before they set. Trim the excess at the top and bottom of all pieces at the same time with a razor blade or the knife supplied with the kit.

8. Cut holes in the paper where the switches and wall plugs fall. Cut these slightly smaller than the covering plates. Replace these plates. Measure any notched-out areas in the wall carefully before cutting the paper.

9. When the job is done you may find small nickel-sized blisters here and there. Slit each blister with a sharp razor blade, apply a little paste under the slit with a toothpick and press down the cut edges of the slit.

10. *Step back and marvel! You have mastered a difficult task! Be sure to tell your friends the story of how you did this task. You deserve their praise.*

5. Minor Plumbing Repairs

This chapter will cover the basics of plumbing—enough to do the necessities which really do not require hiring a plumber.

Note: In an emergency situation you *must* know how to turn off the main water source as well as the individual fixture (sink, tub). This is usually a big valve located next to the home water meter. In an apartment it could be located anywhere in the apartment or even in the basement of the building. If in doubt, check with your building superintendent.

YOUR EQUIPMENT

Here is a list of things which you should find useful.

A wrench. As mentioned in Chapter 1, an adjustable or crescent wrench for removing fittings and trap plugs is a necessity.

Force cup. This unfailing tool, so aptly named the "plumber's helper," is used for unstopping plugged drains.

Dissolving products. These are available in super-markets and hardware stores. They are poured down the drain to help dissolve matter which may be clogging the drain.

Faucet washers. These usually come packaged in basic sizes.

washer

Pipe compound and plumber's string. Compound comes in a tube. The string and compound are used to repair leaky pipe fittings. More details come later in the chapter.

Plumber's snake. This is a long cable that can be fed into drains to free an exceptionally stubborn clog.

SINKS

The stopped-up sink.   Periodically it is advisable to use a dissolving product to flush out and clean grease and accumulation from all the drains in your house. Follow the instructions on the container carefully. Use of these products discourages future drain clogs and insures cleaner, germ-free drains.

However, sometimes clogs are unavoidable. If the water will not drain out of the bowl of your sink, here are the steps you may take to remedy the situation.

1. The first and simplest step is to be sure the lint trap in the drain is clear of hair, chunks of soap or food crumbs.

2. If this is not the problem, try one more quickie thing. Reach through the water and place the palm of your hand over the open drain. Push your palm up and down, making a slight suction. This may start the water draining. However, the solution may be more difficult.

3. The drainpipe may be clogged near the sink bowl or beyond the trap toward the never-never land of pipe and wall. Jam a rag into the overflow opening in the bowl of the sink and remove the lint trap or sink strainer if there is one. Be sure that there are two or three inches of water in the sink.

Position the plumber's helper over the open drain. Hold the wooden handle in both hands and press it down suddenly to create a suction. Do this squish-squish action about a dozen times. This may break up the clog. Using the plumber's helper at the first sign of a sluggish drain will help to prevent more serious problems.

4. If Step 3 fails, try to clean out the drainpipe. Place an empty pail on the floor under the elbow beneath the sink. Unscrew the plug from beneath this elbow trap or, if there is no plug, remove the whole trap by loosening the two fittings on either side of the curving elbow. Use your adjustable

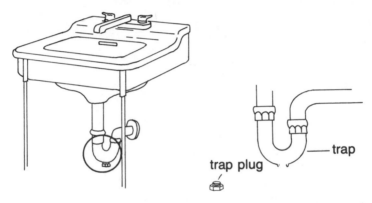

trap

trap plug

wrench for this. Be careful because water and debris may come out with a whoosh when this plug or elbow trap is removed. Be sure the empty pail is carefully positioned underneath. If nothing more than a trickle comes out, the clog is somewhere between the elbow and the sink itself. With a straightened wire coat hanger, poke and probe around through the elbow plug hole and try to dislodge anything which might be causing the stoppage. If this works, flush out the drain with clear hot water.

5. If none of these solutions works and you're still determined, you can invest in a plumber's snake.

This is a long cable (eight feet in length should be adequate) which you feed down the sink drain toward the obstruction. Use it as directed on the package. If this too fails, call the plumber.

The leaky fitting.   Another frequent plumbing ailment is a leaking trap plug. There will be a steady blop, blop on the floor each time you drain the sink and a sad stain will appear on the floor below the plug. The remedy is quite simple.

1. After placing an empty pail or pot on the floor under the elbow joint unscrew the plug with your wrench.

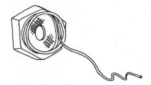

2. Coat the threads of the screw part with pipe compound. Wrap the threads once around with plumber's string, coat the plug again with compound and replace it. The string will swell when it becomes wet and seal the fitting tightly. This same theory can be used to tighten any threaded pipe fitting.

SHOWER HEAD

If the head of your shower spurts water in many different directions or if water dribbles from it but the water pressure is strong, the head probably needs a good cleaning. With time the little holes in the head get clogged.

Shower heads come in quite a variety but usually there is one large nut which attaches to the head of the pipe. Wrapping a rag around this nut to protect it, remove the nut with your adjustable wrench, thus removing the shower head. Soak the head in a grease and dirt dissolver and scrub it with a brush. Then replace the head.

FAUCETS

Replacing a washer.   Faucets used to be fairly standard, and most of the standard types are still in use today although there have been several improved designs in recent years. I'll use the old standard as my example because the basic theory is the same.

If your faucet drips from the spout, whether it be a mixing faucet (hot and cold from one spout) or individual hot and cold taps, chances are the washer is worn out. Here's how to replace it.

1. Buy some assorted washers or a prepackaged assortment from the hardware store.

2. Turn off the water source for the faucet you are fixing. This is usually a valve or two valves (hot and cold) located under the sink or close by the tub. Occasionally in an apartment these valves are located near a sink or tub and will turn off the water throughout the apartment. After you have turned off the valves turn on the faucet in question to be sure the water won't run.

3. With a screwdriver, unscrew the handle screw.

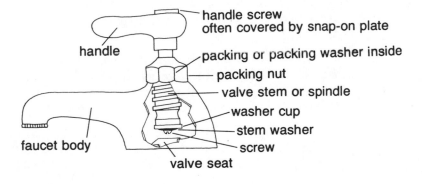

Note that some faucets have a small decorative plate covering this screw. It may say "H" or "C" on it. You can pry up or unscrew this to remove it. Some handles have no handle screw but are pulled straight up and off with force.

4. Wrap tape or a rag around the packing nut (to avoid gouging it) and loosen this nut with your adjustable wrench. You will see packing (string and/or a washer) inside this nut. Leave this all intact. I'll explain about this in detail later. Occasionally on decorative faucets this packing nut is covered by a bell-shaped housing. This housing is held by a flat nut on top. Remove this nut with your wrench and slide the housing off. Now you can loosen the packing nut. Remove this nut along with the valve stem or spindle. Once the nut is loosened this unit removes quite easily.

5. As you hold the stem or spindle you will see at the bottom a small brass screw holding the worn

washer. With a screwdriver remove the screw and scrape the old washer from the stem with a paring knife or nut pick.

6. From your assortment of washers, select a new one which is the same size as the old. Put everything back in place in the reverse order from which you removed it. This should solve most faucet drips.

7. If the faucet continues to leak after the new washer has been installed, chances are the valve seat is nicked or scratched and needs regrinding. If you

care to do this yourself, inexpensive seat-dressing tools are available in most hardware stores. It is a simple operation and the tool will last a lifetime. Follow the directions which come with the tool.

The leaking stem.   If water is leaking around the stem just below the handle it usually means that the faucet must have new packing in the packing nut.

1. To eliminate this leak, first try tightening the packing nut with an adjustable wrench. Put tape or a rag around the nut to protect the chrome. Often a slight turn is all that's needed to stop this leak.

2. If this does not take care of the leak or if after tightening the packing nut you cannot turn on the faucet easily, you must replace the packing.

3. To replace the packing, turn off the water (see Step 2 in the Washer section). Wrap tape or a rag around the packing nut and undo this nut with a wrench.

4. Inside this nut you will probably find a rubber washer and a dirty old piece of string. Change the washer if it's worn and replace the string by winding new pipe string a few times around the thread in the packing nut. Add pipe compound and put the whole thing back together.

The faucet I have described in this section is called a globe faucet. The same principles are used in most standard faucets. If yours does not look like the above description and picture, take it to your hardware dealer. Unless he's grumpy he should be happy to help you. If he's grumpy don't deal there.

TOILET AND TANK

If you carefully lift off the lid (watch it, it's heavy and breakable) from the large ceramic tank behind your toilet bowl you will see a very complicated-looking array of mechanisms. With the lid off, flush the toilet and watch these mechanisms carefully. You will see that the whole arrangement works simply and logically to achieve its purpose. When you flush the handle, the stopper ball lifts, forcing the water swiftly into the toilet bowl, around the edges of the bowl, through the drainpipe and out the outlet pipe.

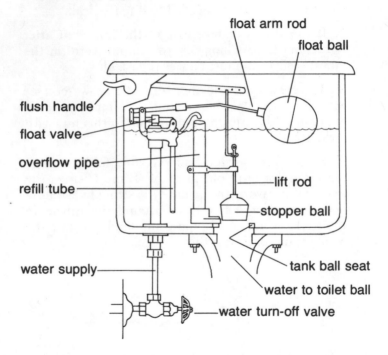

The most common problem with your toilet will be a leak. You can usually hear the leaking water running if you listen carefully. This can be caused by any of several factors. Either the stopper ball, the float ball or the float valve may need adjusting or replacing.

The stopper ball.   If water continues to run into the toilet bowl after flushing and the tank doesn't fill with
water, check the stopper ball as follows:

1. Look into the tank at the stopper ball and jiggle
the flush handle. Is the stopper ball positioned directly over the tank ball seat? If not, the lift rod
may be bent. Straighten it and now see if the stopper

ball falls properly. If the lift rod is bent beyond
repair replace it with a new one. They're usually
neatly prepackaged and inexpensive.

2. The actual stopper ball may be worn and need
replacing. Turn off the water, using the valve under
or behind the bowl, or tie up the float arm so that
the water flow stops. A simple way to do this is to
place a stick of wood or a broom handle across
the top of the open tank and tie the float arm to the
stick.

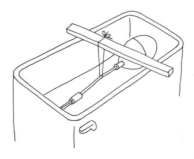

3. Unscrew the stopper ball from the lift rod. Take it to the hardware store and get a new one the same size. It should cost under two dollars.

4. Take some fine steel wool and rub around the tank ball seat to scour it clean. Then screw on the new stopper ball and turn on the water. Your toilet should now be working properly again.

The float ball.   If the tank is filling properly but water continues to run into the toilet bowl after flushing, the float mechanism may be at fault.

1. Lift the float arm to see if the leaking water stops. If it does you either need a new float ball or the float arm needs adjusting. Note that the water level in the tank may not be correct. It should be within one inch of the overflow pipe. If the water level is lower than this, bend the float arm upward slightly. If the water level is high and sloshes over the overflow pipe, bend the float arm downward slightly.

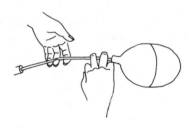

2. If adjusting the arm fails, you need to replace the float ball. Either turn off the toilet's water or tie up the float arm (see Step 3 in the Stopper Ball section).

3. Unscrew the float ball from the float arm, take it to the hardware store and replace it with a new float ball. If this solves the problem, it means that the float ball was leaking and no longer floated, in spite of its name.

The float valve and arm.   If you have tried bending the float arm and water still runs, the float valve needs fixing or replacing.

The purpose of this valve is to shut off the flow of water in the tank after the float ball reaches the proper height. If it doesn't do its job, water will continue to rise and will escape out the overflow pipe.

1. Turn off the water.

2. On most models the float valve has two thumb screws or pins which must be removed first.

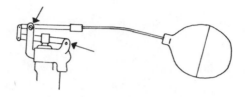

3. The entire float arm mechanism will now be free, including the linkage at the top of the float valve, and you can lift out the whole unit.

4. On the underside of the unit you will see a leatherlike washer either held by a single screw in the center or fitted by force into the recessed area at the bottom. Most models have an additional washer or o-ring which fits around the outside of the plunger. Replace both of these washers.

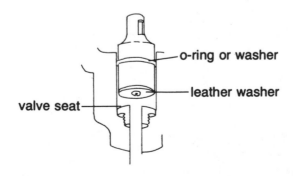

5. With steel wool, remove any rust or corrosion from the float valve. If it is very badly corroded and breaks up or falls apart in your hand or the valve seat inside seems badly worn, replace the whole unit. It will cost a few dollars but will operate well for many years.

6. Return all parts to their former position and turn on the water. Your leaking toilet problems should now be over.

If you have a toilet without a tank, your repairs will unfortunately have to be left to the plumber. It is a vacuum system and many of the parts must be replaced as units.

The clogged toilet bowl.   Your two-year-old niece is visiting and decides to give her Raggedy Ann doll swimming lessons. One innocent flush and Raggedy Ann, doubled over in the drainpipe, creates the biggest flood your bathroom has ever seen.

1. Turn off the water and grab towels, newspapers, anything and sop the water off the floor as quickly as possible! Fast action here can save a lot of grief in the room below.

2. If Raggedy Ann is visible, fine. Reach in and haul her out. But if she's gone too far . . .

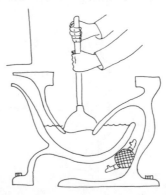

3. Use the dauntless plumber's helper with the same squish-squish action you use on your sink. If this too fails,

4. Try a closet auger, the shortened version of the plumber's snake. Considerable pressure may have to be used to squeeze the auger around the sharp curves of the drainpipe opening.

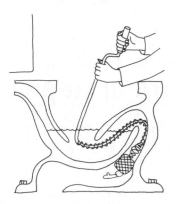

5. Naturally, if the above two methods must be used, explain to your niece that Raggedy Ann has gone to a better world, take her by the hand and buy her a new one—cheap enough investment for a two-year-old's great loss. (Make sure you buy one that already knows how to swim.)

Replacing a toilet seat.   If your toilet seat is worn out it's easy to replace. Buy a new one of your choice (the replacement bolts are interchangeable on most seats).

Feel underneath the area where your seat hinges and attaches to the bowl and you will find two bolts on either side. These are screwed into threaded posts. With an adjustable wrench remove these bolts and the old seat will lift away. Replace it with the new one and tighten the bolts.

6. Simple Basic Electrical Repairs

Most women know very little about the don'ts of electricity. As a result, I will start this chapter by listing some of them.

1. Never turn an electric switch (radio, light, razor, etc.) on or off while you are in the bathtub. And never hold a plugged-in appliance when in the bathtub. *You could be electrocuted!*

2. This warning also applies to soaking those tired feet and turning on a lamp to read the paper. Turn the lamp on *first*. Then soak your feet.

3. It also includes sloshing around outdoors through rain puddles without rubber boots, waving an electric hedge clipper (or mower, edger, etc.).

4. Never remove a light bulb from its socket and then poke something into the socket (especially something like your finger).

5. Never poke anything except a plug into a wall socket for any reason whatsoever.

6. Never use water to put out a fire in an appliance which is plugged in. Unplug the appliance and then use a chemical fire extinguisher. Small ones are avail-

able for under five dollars. You should have at least one.

7. Unplug an item by pulling out the plug itself, not by yanking on the cord. I'm sure you've heard this one before. Don't ignore it. The life of the cord depends on it and you could otherwise get a nasty shock.

8. Turn off the TV set during an electrical storm. Friends of mine had a bad fire in their TV when lightning struck the roof antenna. It ruined the set. My friends now unplug the set when they go away for a weekend. Far-fetched you say? No. They learned a lesson.

9. *Never* put a TV or radio in a position where air cannot circulate around it. It can overheat and cause itself damage.

10. *Never* replace a damaged fuse with anything but a new fuse.

11. *Never* run an extension cord over radiators or heating pipes. Heat will dry and crack the cord and could cause a short circuit.

12. *Always* when working on electrical switches or base plugs shut off the power to that switch!

13. *Don't* run cords under rugs. A bad fire can result if there is a short circuit in the cord.

With these precautions in mind, now read what you can do with electricity.

CIRCUIT BREAKERS AND FUSES

Look around your apartment. On some wall, usually up high, you will see a little metal door (in a house, this will be in the basement). Upon opening this door you will see one of two things:

Either fuses which look like this

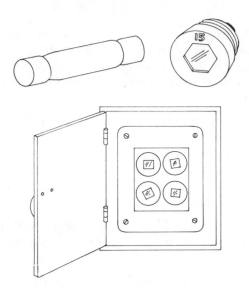

or circuit breakers which look like this.

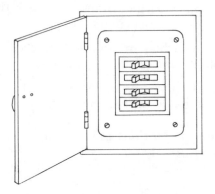

These are safety valves for your electrical power. If you have too many appliances on a circuit or if you are using a defective, short-circuiting appliance, the fuse will blow, killing the power and preventing any serious electrical damage. Replacing the fuse or contacting the circuit breaker without correcting the initial fault will only result in another blowout. This may happen frequently in older dwellings where inadequate wiring exists for our many modern appliances. As a result, when you watch TV with a lamp lit and you decide to iron clothes . . . Woomph! Darkness.

Fuse box. If yours is a fuse box, keep extra fuses on hand. Climb up and look at the fuse sizes. Most household fuses have a glass window and are threaded to screw into position. On the fuse will be the number 15 or maybe 20 (amps). Do not try to put a fuse of a different size in place of a blown one. Use the same size as the one blown.

If you have a large appliance like an electric range or clothes dryer there will probably be a cartridge-type fuse along with the others. Changing these cartridge fuses is best left to a licensed electrician.

Most fuses blow at night, when more power is being used, so know where your flashlight is.

1. When the fuse blows, grope your way over to the flashlight and unplug the offending appliance (usually the last one turned on before the blow).

2. Get your spare fuses and open the fuse box door.

3. When you shine the flash on the fuses you'll see one with its little glass window all black and burned looking. Replace this fuse with its new corresponding size.

4. If after unplugging the suspected appliance the new fuse blows again, the problem may be in the house wiring. Call in a licensed electrician.

5. If, as far as you can see, none of the screw-in fuses look burned out and if *all* the power in your quarters is out it could be that the main fuse has blown. Replacing this is best left to a professional. In an apartment house this fuse is often located in the basement of the building.

Circuit breakers.   This is a newer and easier way of protecting the wiring. Open the door of the box and you will see a series of switches. When a circuit is overloaded, the particular switch regulating that circuit will automatically be thrust open, breaking the circuit. After you have remedied the overloading, flick the switch over to the closed position.

It might be handy to put a gummed label by each fuse or circuit breaker saying what appliance or room is on each one. This could be a big timesaver if that fuse should blow.

PLUGS, SOCKETS
AND GROUNDING DEVICES

If you have purchased an electric drill, you will see that the drill plug has three prongs instead of the usual two. This is a safety measure used on many power tools and some appliances. Plug receptacles in newer homes will accept three-pronged plugs. You can plug these three-pronged tools into your older home wall outlet in two ways.

1. Use an extension cord with two prongs on one end and a three-holed socket on the other.

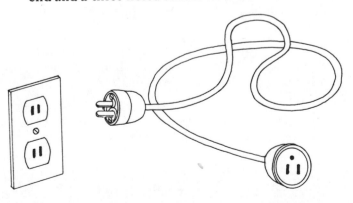

2. Buy a three-hole adapter with a ground wire. Attach the small grounding wire to the small center screw on the wall-outlet plate as shown here. Don't worry. Unless something is wrong with the wall outlet you will not get a shock.

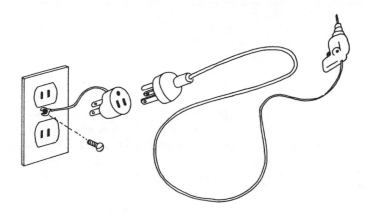

Rewiring a plug.   If an appliance or lamp doesn't work and the trouble isn't something obvious like a burned-out light bulb, check the prongs on the plug.

1. Perhaps you are not getting proper contact in the wall outlet. Bend the two prongs in the plug slightly apart (not together) to obtain a firmer fit and better contact.

2. If this is unsuccessful, face the plug toward you (after unplugging it of course) and make sure that the wires inside have not worked loose from the terminal screws. If this has happened, look at another plug, loosen the screws and reset the wires, copying the second plug. Tighten the screws.

3. If the prongs of the plug are loose, if the small wires in the plug are split or broken, if the plug casing is broken or cracked or if the cord is broken or exposed near the plug, replace the plug.

A. With the cord unplugged, cut off the plug and at least an inch of cord, removing all the broken or cracked portion of the cord.

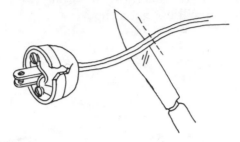

B. Strip off the insulation for about two inches from the end of the cord. Do this carefully so that when the two individual wires are exposed, their insulation is not damaged. (You may want to purchase a tool which easily strips the insulation.)

If the cord looks like two wires with rubber molded over them, split the two sections apart for about two inches.

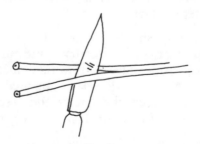

C. Strip off about ½ to ¾ inch of insulation from each wire with a sharp knife or a wire stripper. This will expose many little wires. Try to keep these little wires bunched together and do not cut into the little wires with that sharp knife.

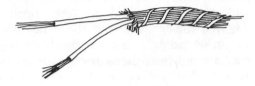

D. Push both wires through the top of the new plug. With the pulled-through wires, tie a special knot called an underwriters' knot in the wire just above the exposed little wires.

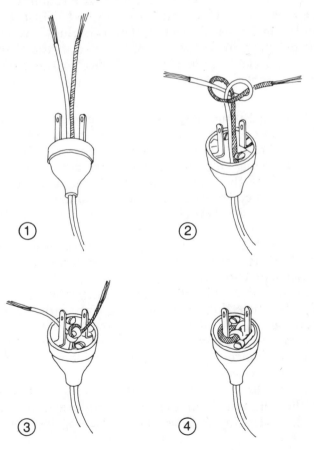

Pull this knot back into the plug, nesting it in between the two prongs. Then loop one wire around one prong and wrap the exposed little wires *clockwise* around the closest terminal screw. Tighten the screw. Wrap the other wire around the other prong and wrap the little wires *clockwise* around the other screw in the same manner. Be sure that neither bunch of little wires touches the other bunch of little wires. Also be certain that each bunch of little wires is gathered under its screw and that no loose strands stick out.

The above steps A–D show the best method of replacing most plugs. However, for lamps and light extension cords you can use the newer clamp-on plugs. Just cut off the old plug, insert the end of the cord in the clamp-on plug and clamp it in place according to the directions that come with the plug.

Female appliance plug (named by a male chauvinist). Many cords have a big, flat plug at one end which fastens directly into a particular appliance (electric coffee maker, frying pan, grill). These plugs take a lot of hard use and as their casings are often made of a brittle material they are easily chipped or broken. Very often the wires inside become worn from pulling the plug in and out.

So don't despair if you think the appliance has gone kerflooey. It may be only this plug. Before running to a serviceman, check the plug yourself.

Be sure the wall outlet you're using is working properly. To prove this, plug a working lamp into the outlet. If the lamp lights, the outlet is working.

If you have a cord like the questionable one from another appliance, try it out on the problem appliance. If the appliance now works, great!

If you have no second cord and plug to test with, unplug the one from the outlet and see if its case is cracked or chipped. Does the cord going into the case seem insecure and loose? Does it look frayed or burned? Check the case and see if its two halves seem loose and wobbly.

If any of these things are so, it's worth investing in a new cord and plug because if it isn't now giving you trouble it soon will. They're not expensive and both five and ten cent stores and hardware stores carry them. If your new plug doesn't remedy the situation, see a serviceman.

A damaged electric cord.   Do not try to repair a heater cord (for toaster, iron, coffee pot or other heating appliances). Have a serviceman replace the cord with a new one.

You can repair a damaged lamp cord or extension cord as follows:

> 1. If only the outer insulation is frayed or broken, wrap the damaged area well with electrical tape.
>
> 2. If the inner wires are damaged too and the cut or break goes deep, cut off the offending area.

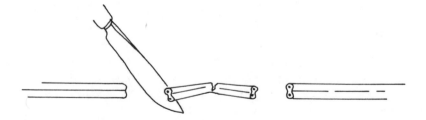

> 3. With a wire stripper or sharp paring knife, strip off about two inches of insulation on each side of the cut.

4. Twist the opposite wires together.

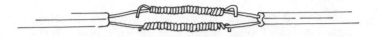

5. Wrap each wire with electrical tape making sure that the tape covers *all* exposed metal wire. In fact, it's a good idea to wrap two layers of tape to be absolutely sure all exposed wire is covered.

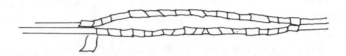

6. Last wrap the two wrapped wires together with more electrical tape. For added safety, wrap a second coat of tape around the item.

WALL SWITCHES

It is actually a simple job to replace a defective wall switch. The most important thing is to shut off the power to that switch. If you don't do this it could kill you!

If after that dire warning you're still game to continue, here's what to do.

1. Shut off the power either by pulling the main switch or by unscrewing the correct fuse. Be sure you *know* it's the correct fuse.

2. As a double safety against a shock, you may want to work with a rubber-handled screwdriver. If you have them, wear sneakers. Never work in bare feet.

Unscrew the two screws from the switch-plate cover and remove the cover. Do *not* do this before the power is shut off.

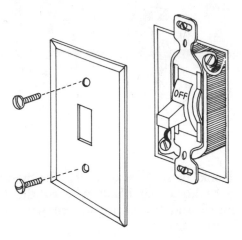

3. Unscrew the two screws at the top and bottom which hold the switch in position against the wall and the switch box.

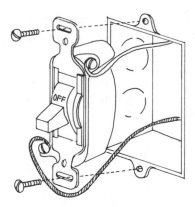

4. After pulling the switch carefully out of the box, you will see that it is tethered by two wires. Unhook these wires by loosening the terminal screws mounted on the switch.

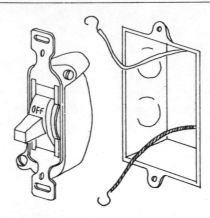

5. Hook these two wires to the new switch. Be sure to hook the black wire to the brass-colored terminal and the white or red wire to the silver-colored terminal.

6. Bend the wires back into the switch box and replace the screws which hold the switch on the wall.

7. Replace the switch plate.

In many newer houses, after you have removed the switch you will see a third wire called a ground wire in the switch box. This wire is frequently green and is usually attached to the back of the switch. If this is true of your switch box check with your hardware store on installation or check the instructions on the packaging.

LAMPS

Rewiring a lamp. Your lamp needs fixing if the light is fluttering or buzzing or if you have to switch it on and off a couple of times before it makes contact.

1. Check the lamp plug as described earlier in the section Rewiring a Plug. If it needs replacing, use

one of the new, easy snap-on varieties. More than likely, however, your problem is in the lamp's socket.

2. Unplug the lamp! Remove the lampshade and bulb. The socket into which the bulb screws has a springy metal tab in it. With a screwdriver, bend this tab slightly upward to make a tighter contact between the tab and the end of the bulb.

Screw in the light bulb, plug in the lamp and try it. It works? Good! But if it doesn't, check the socket.

3. Unplug the lamp! Remove the bulb again. Pull the shell apart from the cap, leaving the cap in position. Be sure the terminal screws around which the wires are wrapped are tight and examine all of the cord to make sure it isn't worn or broken anywhere (if the cord needs replacing, see the section Replacing the Lamp Cord). Put the lamp together again and try it. If there is still no light, the switch may be faulty and you need to replace the socket.

Replacing the socket

1. Unplug the lamp! Pull the socket shell from the cap, leaving the cap in position. If the old cord is not broken you may proceed, using the existing cord. Loosen the two terminal screws inside the socket and remove each wire. Throw the old socket away.

2. Pull apart the new socket to reveal the terminal screws. Discard the new cap part as it is interchangeable with the old cap already in position. Trying to remove the old cap can loosen the whole lamp mechanism. If at all possible, leave the old cap.

3. Twist each wire clockwise around each terminal screw, taking care to match the dark wire to the bronze-colored screw and the light (or red) wire to the aluminum-colored screw.

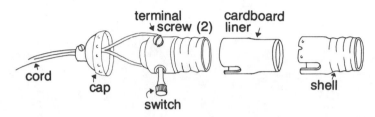

light socket

Put the socket shell back on the cap. Do not forget the cardboard liner as it is protection against short circuits. Pull the cord gently at the bottom of the lamp to make it taut.

4. Replace the bulb and plug in your lamp as good as new.

Replacing the lamp cord.   Is the cord damaged inside the body of the lamp or between the lamp and the plug? Does the light flicker when the cord is wriggled? Play it safe and replace the full cord as well as the socket.

1. Unplug the lamp! Unscrew the bulb and remove the harp. (This is the curved wire section that holds on the lampshade. It usually squeezes in and pulls upward to remove.) Pull apart the shell of the socket from the cap. Unscrew the old wires from the two terminals. A smart move at this point would be to tie a long string onto the top of the old lamp cord.

You'll understand as you read on. Discard all the old parts: the old switch, plug, socket.

Pull the cord out through the bottom of the lamp. The string will remain inside the lamp, sticking out from the top. Untie the string from the old cord. Tie on the new cord and from the top of the lamp, pull the string, drawing the new cord through the lamp.

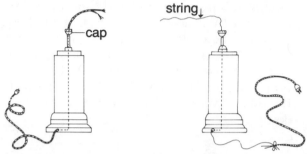

2. Using wire strippers, strip off about three quarters of an inch of insulation at the top end of the lamp cord, revealing the two bunches of small wires. Twist each bunch of wires tightly together, making two tight bunches. Wrap the bunch from the black wire clockwise around the dark terminal screw of the new socket. Wrap the bunch from the white (or red) wire clockwise around the light terminal screw. Reassemble the socket and shell onto the lamp cap as described in Step 3 in the previous section.

All the information in this section should give you hints on how to convert an antique gas lamp or a handsome vase into a lamp. Go to an electrical supply store or a good hardware store and look around at the kits, supplies and instruction booklets which are available.

Fluorescent lamps. An incandescent lamp lights by heating a tungsten filament inside a bulb until it glows bright white hot. The fluorescent lamp is a tube of glass filled with mercury vapor or gas. When heated this gas gives off ultraviolet light which transmits itself to a phos-phorescent coating on the inside of the tube, which in turn glows brightly.

The fluorescent lamp has basically three parts with which you need be concerned.

1. The tube itself. This tube exerts most of its energy when you turn it on. Therefore, frequent turning on, off and on again is the most wearing opera-tion. If a tube does a great deal of blinking, it is using its energy too rapidly. To preserve the tube, this blinking should be remedied promptly. It could be that the two pins in the ends of the tube are not firmly mounted in the sockets. Check this first. Hold the tube in your hand so that the pins align up and down.

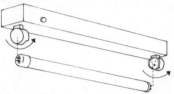

Push both ends into their corresponding sockets and twist the tube a quarter-turn in the socket in the direction indicated by the arrows in the above drawing. This locks the tube into the sockets.

If the blinking persists, your next concern is . . .

2. The starter. This is the little metal cylinder near one end of the fixture. If the tube lights at both ends but is dim in the middle, the starter is probably the culprit. Remove it by pressing down upon it and turning it to one side until it comes out. Starters, though resembling one another, have varied ratings so take yours to the hardware store to be sure you replace it with one of the same rating.

3. The sockets are the third items with which you should be concerned. Turn off the power or unplug the lamp. Be sure that the sockets are firm. Tighten the screws which hold the socket to the metal fixture.

A fluorescent tube will have a much longer life than an incandescent bulb. When the tube begins to darken at the ends it is nearing the end of its life. Don't be hasty in replacing it as it still has many hours to go. But if checking the sockets and replacing the starter fail to stop the winking and fluttering, it does mean that in spite of its loyal service the bulb is going to have to be replaced.

FLASHLIGHTS

When it works, we take it for granted. When it doesn't we curse it. If you've changed the batteries and still, no light, take a look at the gizzards of the flashlight. There's probably a simple explanation.

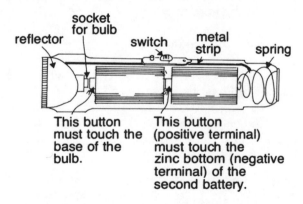

socket for bulb · reflector · switch · metal strip · spring

This button must touch the base of the bulb.

This button (positive terminal) must touch the zinc bottom (negative terminal) of the second battery.

1. Check to be sure your batteries are loaded in the correct position.

2. Check the bulb and replace it if needed.

3. If the light is dim, rub the positive terminal (brass button) on each battery with fine sandpaper or emery paper. This will clean them for sharper contact. Also rub the terminal mounted under the bulb socket. Clean the spring at the bottom of the flash and stretch it out slightly.

4. If the light winks, clean and slightly stretch out the spring in the light's base. Be sure the metal switch strip running along the side of the flash touches the reflector and that the reflector is in position firmly.

Flashlights come in all shapes and sizes but the above explanation can be adapted to them all.

MAINTAINING MOTORS AND APPLIANCES

When you purchase an appliance it is wise to hold on to the literature included in the packing. This generally tells how to maintain the item and, if it should require oiling, how and where to oil it.

1. Oiling. If you do oil any appliance which requires it, *keep the oiling to a minimum.* One or two drops in each oil hole is all that's required. Don't think you're doing a good deed by oiling many areas of an electric motor. Oil *only* where instructions indicate. A great deal of damage can be done to an electric motor by drowning it in oil or oiling the wrong places.

2. Cleanliness. If an appliance is used where it can pick up a great deal of lint, be sure to keep the works clean by brushing them with a dry paint brush or vacuuming them. Even a good, strong burst from your own lungs will help a bit. Lint and fluff which accumulate make a serious fire hazard. Dirt and grit collecting in a motor are abrasive and can wear down moving parts badly. Clean these out using the same methods.

3. If you suspect that the brushes in an electric motor are worn, take the appliance to a repairman to have them replaced.

7. Doors and Windows

THE WINDOW WON'T OPEN

One of the most frustrating encounters in life is between you and a window that won't open. Don't get involved in a wrestling match with it. You'll only end up with a broken window, a sheepish look and maybe a cut hand.

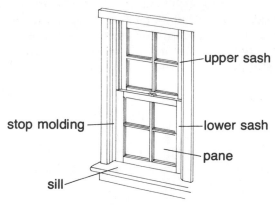

Usually a wooden window is stuck because someone (not you of course) has painted it and as the paint was drying, has let the window stay in one position too long. Or maybe just plain dampness has swelled the wood. To unstick it proceed as follows:

81

1. If the window is merely stiff, rub a wad of paraffin or a thick candle up and down the tracks where the window sticks against the frame.

2. If it is really stuck, tap all around with a putty knife slid between the edge of the sash and the stop molding as shown. Just tap the putty knife, don't aim and swing the hammer. Chances are you'll miss if you try. *Do not* use a screwdriver instead of a putty knife. You'll damage the wood badly.

3. If this doesn't jar the sash free more drastic measures can be taken. If possible work from the outside. Tap a hatchet or ax head gently into the crack where the window sash meets the sill. Lift the hatchet gently as you move along the sill. Be careful not to mar the woodwork.

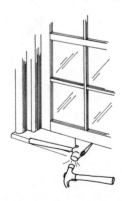

4. When the window has been raised, scrape accumulated paint from around the edge and sand with sandpaper. If the window has stuck from swelling this can often be remedied by rapping the stop molding with a piece of wood and a hammer after the window has been fully raised. Go up and down both sides, rapping as much of the frame as you can to try to regain the original shape.

5. Some older windows use a pulley system of sash weights and cords to open and close the window. In time these cords break and should be replaced with more durable chains. If your window opens with difficulty or slams shut by itself, this could be the problem. You can do this job but I would advise calling a professional.

A BROKEN WINDOW
IN A WOODEN FRAME

It's best to work in this project from the outside but this may be difficult if you're on the seventeenth floor with nothing but air between you and the sidewalk. It is possible to install a new piece of glass from the inside reaching out though it is extremely awkward and difficult.

1. Wearing the heaviest gloves you own, or wearing lighter gloves and using pot holders, carefully remove all broken glass from the window. If the old putty is hard and the glass is held tight, rock the glass to and fro to break the seal. Then pull it straight out toward you. Hammer out small glass chips in the old putty gently with hammer and chisel. Be careful of your eyes as you do this because chips may fly. If you have eye glasses, wear them. Otherwise it would be smart to wear sunglasses for protection.

2. When all the glass is out, you will see a groove running around the frame where the glass sat. Remove all old, dried putty from this groove with a narrow chisel or screwdriver. Take care not to gouge into the frame while doing this.

3. As you are removing the old putty you probably will encounter some glazier's points. These are small metal triangles used to hold the glass in position:

△   (actual size). These may be pulled out with pliers. If you're careful not to bend them, you can reuse them with the new glass.

4. After all putty and glazier's points have been removed, paint the groove with thinned-down outdoor paint. This "primer" protects the wood from damp-

ness and will insure a good bond between glass and glazing compound (putty).

5. Measure the opening to determine the size glass needed. Take this information to a glass cutter. Be sure to tell him that this is the *exact size* of the opening. He will cut the glass slightly smaller to allow for the give and take a window frame must endure in wind and heavy weather. Very often he will cut the glass while you wait.

6. Apply a thin portion of glazing compound (⅛ to ¼ inch thick) around the groove in which the glass is to rest. Holding the glass by the edges, press it firmly into this bedding of putty (compound) and tap the glazier's points in flush with the glass. You can tap these in quite easily by laying the flat edge of a screwdriver against the flat edge of the point and tapping the screwdriver with a hammer.

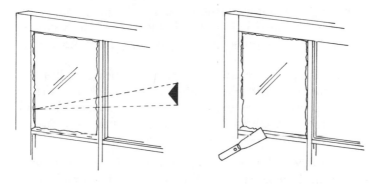

On a large pane of glass, glazier's points should be spaced about nine inches apart. On a small-sized windowpane, one on top, one on the bottom and two on either side should be adequate.

7. Apply glazing compound to the inside as extra insurance. Using a putty knife, smooth the putty out neatly at a bevel, following one of your other windows as an example.

STEEL CASEMENT WINDOWS

The most common ailment with steel casement windows that begin to act stubbornly is rust. The window will not open or it will fail to close snugly. If the window won't open, proceed as follows.

1. Buy some deep-penetrating oil and apply this to all moving parts of hinges and handles. Let it soak in well for about fifteen minutes.

2. Try opening the window after this penetration of oil. If it still won't budge, hold a block of wood against the frame and rap it with a hammer.

3. If the window still doesn't open, it has probably been painted shut. Use the putty-knife-and-hammer combination described in Step 1 of the previous section.

Once the window is open you should take some preventive measures so that it will swing open and closed freely. Here is the procedure for painting and lubricating.

1. Scrape all rusty areas clean. Chip off all flaky paint and rust and scrub the metal frames with a wire brush. On stubborn areas, especially around hinges, use emery paper (similar to fine sandpaper) or medium steel wool.

2. Check the condition of the glazing compound around each pane. If the compound is cracked or dry, replace it. First scrape off the old putty, baring the metal window frame where the glass sets. Paint this bare metal with red lead, a priming paint which is rust-resistant. This is the brick-red-colored paint you often see on metal surfaces. Then apply fresh glazing compound. Be sure it is metal casement putty.

3. When you're sure the surfaces of the steel frame are relatively smooth and that no old paint drips are interfering with the window operation, paint the entire frame with red lead. When this has thoroughly dried, give the window frames a coat of paint of the desired color. Ask your paint dealer what type of paint to buy. As the paint dries, move the window every once and a while to keep it from binding.

4. Lubricate all moving parts (latches, hinges, handles) with household oil. Do this automatically each spring and fall.

ALUMINUM WINDOW MAINTENANCE

These windows need no paint but it is desirable to give them a coat of wax occasionally. A good paste auto wax works well. Wax them often, as weather causes them to pit. For a broken window in a steel or aluminum window frame, follow the same procedures as described for wooden-frame windows. Use glazing compound for steel windows and substitute glazing clips for glazier's points.

REPLACING SCREENING

If you'd like to feel the summer breezes but not the summer soot and bugs, it's an easy matter to replace the worn-out screening on your old wooden screens.

If the frames are in good shape but the screening is rusted or torn, here's how to proceed.

1. Carefully pry off the molding around the screen so that it can be reused.

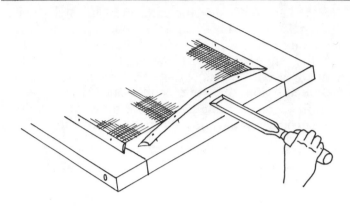

2. Remove the old, worn screening by taking out all the tacks holding it in place.

3. If the screen frame and molding need repainting this is a good time to do it. The screening is off and you don't have to worry about getting paint on it.

4. You may choose from among a variety of screening materials. I would advise fiber glass as it's easy to cut and install and never needs painting. It usually comes in a standard width and is sold by the yard in length.

5. Measure and cut the screening with a ruler and heavy scissors. Allow ½ inch extra material on all sides. This will be folded under as a hem to assure a stronger grip and will eventually be covered by the molding.

6. Starting on a long side, fold the mesh over ½ inch as mentioned in Step 5. Staple the mesh to the frame at the two corners, then at the center and then at about 1-inch intervals in between.

7. Go to the opposite long edge and, pulling the screen taut, hem and staple those two corners, then the center, then at 1-inch intervals.

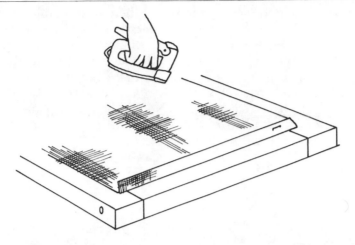

8. Pulling the screening taut, fasten the two short sides.

9. Replace the moldings in the same positions as they had been, nailing them into position with new wire brads.

You can also replace screening in an aluminum combination storm-and-screen window.

1. Remove the plastic spine from the groove at the screen area.

2. Cut a piece of screening the size of the outer edges of the window frame.

3. Cut off the corners of the new screen at a 45-degree angle, leaving enough material at the corner to tuck into the groove.

4. Lay the screen on top of the window's frame. As you force the plastic spine into its groove pull the mesh taut. Then lightly tap the spine well into the groove with a hammer.

5. With a razor, trim off the extra screening material that hangs outside the screen.

If you live in an apartment and there is no visible way to hang the screens, here is a suggestion. Buy four hooks and eyes, attach the eyes to the window frame and the hooks to the screen (using the threaded awl to start the holes). The fit may not be as accurate as if you'd used the proper hardware but unless you're a perfectionist it will probably satisfy you. Note that this screen fits into the bottom half of the window with the upper window sash flush with the screen top.

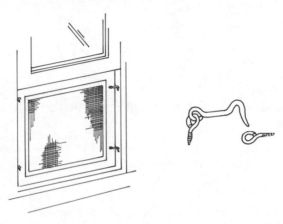

If your old metal screening doesn't need replacing but does have a couple of holes that need repairing, here's how to proceed.

1. If the wires are only pulled apart try straightening them out with a small nail or an ice pick.

2. If the screening is broken, you can buy small screen patches at the hardware store. Follow the directions on the packet. The patches are easy to attach.

If your screening is made of fiber glass, you can mend a small puncture by fusing a fiber-glass patch to the screening by applying heat.

1. Hold something metal like the bottom of a pot to the back side of the screen.

2. From a scrap of fiber-glass screening, cut a patch slightly larger than the hole to be mended.

3. Hold the patch against the screening and run the tip of a hot iron around the edges until they melt slightly and stick tight. Make a couple of practice runs on scrap material before you do the actual job.

4. Sew the plastic screening patches into place with nylon thread.

If the screening is somewhat rusted but only badly enough to look unsightly:

1. Lay it flat and scrub both sides with a stiff brush.

2. Scrub both sides with soap and water, rinse and let dry.

3. Paint both sides of the screening with spray varnish or spray paint. To avoid clogging, spray two light coats rather than one heavy one. If you use paint from a can, paint it on using an old piece of carpet. This will help avoid clogging.

If the frame of the screen is wobbly, brace each corner with angle irons. Mark the screw holes on the screen frames with a pencil. Make pilot holes with the threaded awl and then screw the angles into position as illustrated.

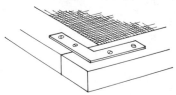

WINDOW SHADES

If your window shades are worn out, you can replace them with anything from five-and-ten-cent-store shades to custom-designed items from that posh little shop on the corner. Or you can easily make your own attractive shades from the colorful and patterned vinyls which are sold by the yard.

1. Remove the old or worn fabric from the shade roller or buy inexpensive shades and remove the fabric. I suspect that if you shopped you could find the rollers by themselves and cut your own stick but it's not much more expensive to buy a reasonably priced, made-up shade.

2. Using the old fabric as a pattern, cut the vinyl to the same size, leaving enough for the stick and hem at the bottom and a fold at the top.

3. Staple the fabric to the roller, giving it a hem lip for strength.

4. Hem and stitch the lower edge, leaving a slot wide enough for the stick.

5. If desired, drill through the vinyl and stick at the center and tie on a shade pull.

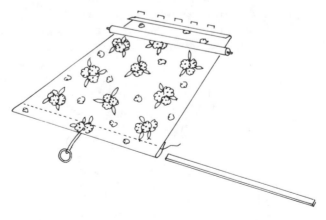

If your window shade is not working properly, try the following remedies before spending any money.

1. If the shade won't roll up all the way it is too loose. Remove it from its brackets, roll it up by hand all the way and replace it onto the brackets.

2. If the shade snaps up violently, it is too tight. Remove it from its brackets and unroll it about half-way by hand. Replace it onto the brackets.

3. If the shade won't catch when it's rolled down, remove it from its brackets and oil the mechanism on the roller. (Don't let oil run onto the fabric).

4. Make sure the brackets are not bent or worn. If they are, try to bend them back into shape with pliers or replace them with new ones.

If you want to tackle your venetian blinds, go to it! New tapes can be bought with instructions for replacing them, new cords can be installed and new slats can even be strung.

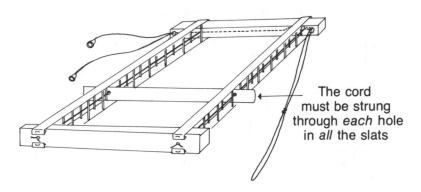

The cord must be strung through *each* hole in *all* the slats

THE DOOR THAT STICKS

You know that door that has been sticking for months and now you're trapped in the bathroom and the phone's ringing. Don't panic. He'll call back. But once you get out, plan to fix that door very soon. Don't haul out your heavy-duty equipment like hammer and saw. Chances are the fixing is of a much more subtle nature.

1. Check the screws in the hinges to be sure none have worked loose. Even a small thing like that is enough to cause the door to be thrown off balance and to bind.

2. If the screws are all secure, try to find out exactly where the door is sticking. This can be determined by taking a thin sheet of cardboard and sliding it between the closed door and the door frame. The trouble spot is where your cardboard will not pass.

3. If the door sticks along the side near the top or at the bottom by the floor, remove the screws of the frame side of the *lower* hinge and insert one or more thicknesses of heavy paper to shim the door outward. If the door should stick at the top outside edge or along the side near the bottom where it opens, shim the *upper* hinge. You can see what I mean by the exaggerated illustrations.

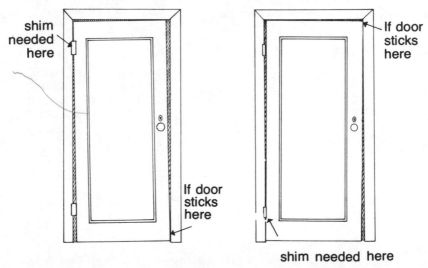

shim needed here

If door sticks here

If door sticks here

shim needed here

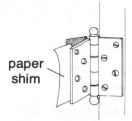

paper shim

4. If shimming the door helped but was not quite effective enough, wrap and staple a piece of coarse sandpaper around a block of wood and sand the area where the sticking occurs.

5. Sometimes a door will stick in several areas due to a build-up of layers of paint. Buy a can of paint remover and, following the directions on the can, strip the paint off to the bare wood or from both faces of the areas that rub together. Sand and repaint the bare wood with a primer and sealer paint; when that is dry, paint the wood the desired color.

6. If there is no paint build-up and the door still sticks along the latch edge in various places, it will have to be trimmed or planed. This can be difficult, and if you don't have the tools and the know-how, call in a pro.

If the latch in the edge of the door does not engage properly with the striker plate in the door frame, the door will not close. Try the following:

1. See if the latch fits cleanly into the striker plate. If not, remove the striker plate and replace it higher

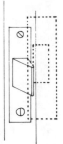

or lower as necessary, or remove the striker plate and, with a metal file, enlarge the hole in the plate where it is necessary.

2. If the striker plate is recessed too deeply into the door frame and the latch won't reach it, remove the plate and insert cardboard shims behind it to bring it out closer to the door latch.

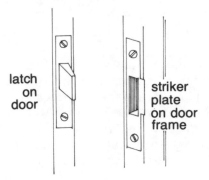

latch on door

striker plate on door frame

WEATHER STRIPPING

On a cold winter night you may feel breezes from the window or from under the door varying from a gentle zephyr to a howling gale. Perhaps even rain is able to ooze its way in. This is not only uncomfortable but costly, as the furnace will work twice as hard as normal. You can correct this problem by fastening weather stripping around your window and door frames.

Weather stripping comes in several styles and a variety of materials—felt, vinyl, plastic, foam and metal, just to name a few.

The metal, rigid style, usually of aluminum, is the most permanent and most professional. But for ease in handling I recommend the flexible type in vinyl or plastic. It lasts well, is easy to cut and fit and looks good. Rustproof nails or tacks are usually included.

For metal doors or windows, a weather strip which comes with an adhesive backing will probably be the most convenient for you.

Follow the directions enclosed with the packaging. Below are illustrated two areas where drafts most frequently occur and how they look when weather stripped.

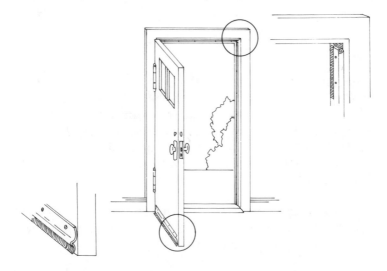

DOORKNOBS

If your doorknob is loose, loosen the set screw in the base of the knob. Turn the knob clockwise until it is firm, then reset the screw.

If it is still loose, again loosen the set screw and pull the knob off the spindle. Or, if it's threaded, turn the knob counterclockwise until it pulls out of its spindle (which is probably worn). Pull out the knob on the opposite side and replace the worn spindle. Turn the knob clockwise and tighten the set screw.

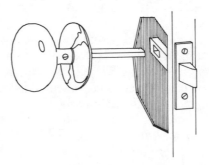

Follow these instructions to replace the knob with a more modern or elaborate fixture.

SAFETY DEVICES

Door latches or locks.   If your key turns stiffly, the lock probably needs a shot of graphite. Graphite powder comes in a plastic squeeze container and literally shoots out when squeezed. Apply the nozzle of the graphite container to the keyhole and then to the latch. Squirt some in and turn the key several times to loosen the lock. If the lock is broken, call the locksmith.

Window locks.   Most windows have their own locks but clever burglars seem to manage to outwit these simple devices. I like additional security.

One of the quickest ways to make your own window lock is to drill a hole into both the inner and outer window frames and then insert a stove bolt. You can also drill a second hole part way up the upper window so that the window may be bolted open or closed.

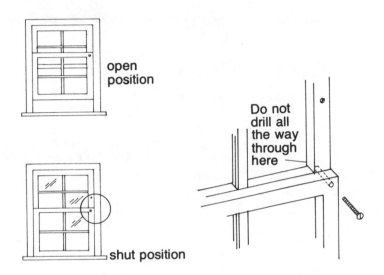

open
position

Do not
drill all
the way
through
here

shut position

I have this simple device in my own apartment and it is quite effective.

There are other devices sold in hardware stores, some fairly worthwhile, some almost useless. Look and decide for yourself.

The most effective burglar-proofing is, of course, bars. But as these are permanent, you cannot get out in case of fire. Therefore I don't advise such drastic measures. In fact most building codes and home and apartment rental leases do not permit them.

Almost as effective is the locked gate. It is unsightly, as it is installed on the inside of the room, but it can be unlocked and swung open in case a fast exit is necessary. Keep the key handy. Again, check your lease; some landlords do not permit the gate either, and it is illegal in some cities.

8. New Floors for Fun and Function

I don't care what your brother-in-law says! Don't listen to him! You *can* install a new floor or fix your old one if you have patience and use care.

DO YOU WANT TO LAY TILES?

If you're considering redoing a floor, go to a tile dealer and look at the infinite variety of handsome patterns available. This will inspire you with enthusiasm. A few years ago, tiles made to look like brick, marble, terra cotta or wood were only mildly successful. Today all these patterns and more are extremely realistic and very durable. Talk to your dealer about vinyl, asbestos, asphalt and cork, and ask what best suits your needs.

Naturally there is an extensive price range, depending upon the realistic look of the pattern and its durability. Most of the tiles made for household uses are slightly thicker than $\frac{1}{16}$ inch. The commercial variety usually runs about $\frac{1}{8}$ inch in thickness. Consult your dealer to be sure that the tiles you have in mind are suitable for your floors.

Some flooring will not accept tiles or sheet vinyl.

1. You cannot install tiles on top of wooden floors which are ripply, broken, springy or loose. The floor-

boards must be under 3 inches in width and the floor must be double-thick. (Most finished floors are of double thickness.) If the flooring is in bad shape or if the boards are too wide, an additional ¼-inch-thick plywood cover must be laid. I'll explain how to do this later.

2. The rules say you cannot install floor tiles on top of old linoleum or tiles. This should be lifted or a false base of plywood put on top. However, if you have a two- or three-year lease and don't care whether the flooring lasts a third of your lifetime, and if your lease says nothing about restrictions of this sort, go ahead and lay the tiles. If the undertile is sturdy and level, you'll do fine for at least five years.

3. You cannot install tiles on a patio or porch which is exposed to bad weather.

4. You cannot install tiles on a concrete floor which has any dampness or sweat. Be sure the floor is reasonably level and dry. If it is damp, get the advice of a professional.

REMEDYING AN UNSUITABLE FLOOR

Concrete floors.   Uneven concrete or quarry (stone slab) floors can be made smooth for tiling.

Use a mastic substance which is poured onto the floor and leveled roughly with a trowel. It then will spread itself evenly to form a smooth, level surface. To fill any holes or expansion joints, a patching compound is available. These products will remedy only minor irregularities.

If the floor is in direct contact with the ground and is painted or varnished, remove as much finish as possible. If the floor is suspended, it will have at least 18 inches of air space under it. Then you may leave the paint or varnish on the surface. The only step necessary is to roughen the surface with a wire brush. If the concrete floor holds dampness or is not particularly level, you'll need professional help.

Wooden floors.   If the floor to be tiled is wood, you're safe when the floorboards are narrow. But, as mentioned earlier, if the boards are 3 inches or wider, you will need added support. (If the floor needs repair, loose boards renailed or broken boards replaced, see the section Repairing a Wood Floor.) The best way to give that added support is to cover the entire floor with ¼-inch plywood. No, no! Come back! Don't be discouraged. It's not that big a job. Usually plywood panels come approximately 4 by 8 feet. They should be laid out in a bricklike fashion so that the continuous seam goes crosswise to the underfloor. The staggered seams which run parallel to the floorboards should be positioned or trimmed so that each butted plywood piece is nailed to the same underfloorboard.

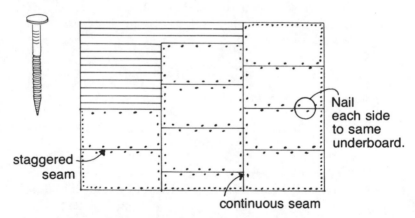

Nail each side to same underboard.

staggered seam

continuous seam

Use spiral flooring nails or ringed nails every 2 inches apart around the edges and every 6 inches apart along the seams (see above diagram).

If any curved cuts are necessary don't be concerned about getting them perfect. Make a paper pattern of the curve, cut it out and transfer it onto the wood. If you

have a curve like this ⌣ and you cut it like this
⌣ that's close enough. For small cuts like these, it would be convenient to buy a keyhole saw.

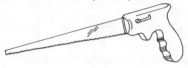

This diagram will show you just how to cut the wood to fit around a pipe.

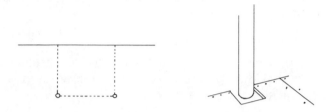

LAYING THE TILES

The following are general instructions for laying most types of tiles. The specific adhesives or materials you use will depend upon the type of tiles you choose. When you buy the tiles, complete instructions will be in the packages, including the type of adhesive necessary.

There is also a very effective self-stick tile on the market. Be sure to inquire about this. It is installed in the same manner as other tiles, eliminating the step of spreading the adhesive. These tiles usually have a removable paper back which protects the adhesive.

The specific tools needed for laying tiles are:

1. A ruler or yardstick for any necessary measuring

2. String and soft chalk for marking the measures

3. Heavy shears or a linoleum knife for cutting tiles

4. A paint roller and tray or a wide (3½- or 4-inch) paintbrush

5. A carpenter's square to be sure of a true 90-degree angle

6. A rolling pin to flatten down the tiles well

At this point you should pry off all floor molding around the room. You must lay the border tiles snugly against the wall and this can only be done by removing the molding. It can later be put back or new molding can be installed. You can buy a special molding which goes with the tiles you have chosen. It is flexible, easy to install and quite handsome.

Begin by dividing the floor into four exact quarters.

1. Ignoring any indents for closets or cutouts for bay windows, on the floor mark the exact midpoint of each of the two long walls.

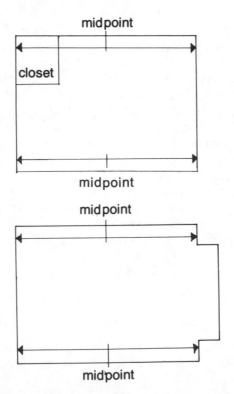

2. Drive a small nail partially into the floor at each of these two center points. Take a long piece of string, coat it heavily with chalk and tie it onto each of the small nails. Then snap the string as you would a bow and arrow onto the floor. The string will transpose a chalk line onto the floor.

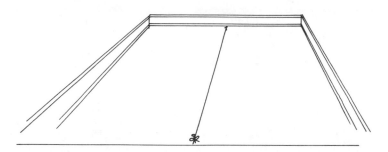

3. Find the center mark on the two shorter walls in the same manner, partially hammer in a nail at each of these two points, tie on the chalked string and *before* you snap this string check the angles to be sure they are square.

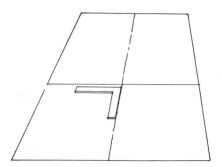

As shown above, hold the square against the chalked line. Then be sure the other straight edge of the square lines up with the newly tied-on string. Now snap the string to mark the perpendicular. You will now have crossed chalk marks in the center of the room which look like this.

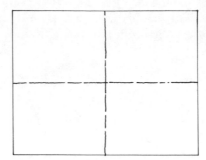

4. The next step is to plan a border of tiles all of equal size around the room like this.

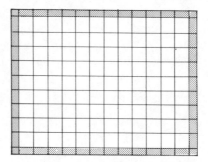

You do *not* want to end up with an unbalanced border like this.

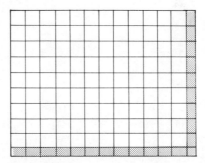

Here's how to proceed.

A. Lay a row of loose, unglued tiles along the chalk lines starting at the center, carefully lining up the first tile against the crossed chalk lines. Lay the loose tiles to each wall until another *full* tile cannot be positioned.

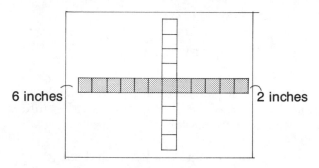

6 inches   2 inches

B. Now shift each row of tiles either to the left or right until the spaces remaining on opposite ends are equal.

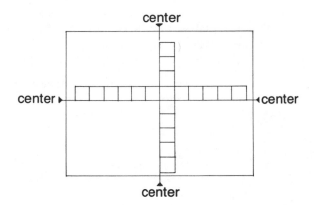

center

center ►   ◄ center

center

C. Now nail and tie new chalked string in the adjusted positions of the tile for your exact starting place. Snap the strings to make new marks and start with the first tile as indicated here.

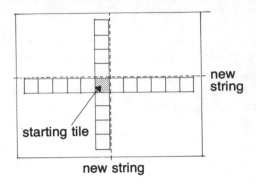

5. There is a particular order recommended for laying tiles. Since the floor is now divided into quarters, work each quarter as a separate unit.

A. Open the can of adhesive and stir it well. Follow the directions on the can for drying time and additional hints.

B. Pour a small amount into the paint tray and roll a thin coat, using the paint roller, over one quarter of the floor. The adhesive may also be painted on with a brush. Be sure to brush it on thinly and evenly. Be careful not to obliterate your chalk guides. They are important to you.

C. Position the first group of tiles over this area in the following sequence.

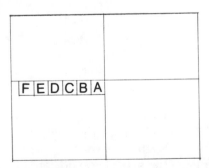

Be very careful to align each tile snugly against the chalk line and butt it firmly against its neighbor. Try hard to lay or drop each tile into position. Do not put it down and slide it over.

D. Your next sequence of tiles should be as follows.

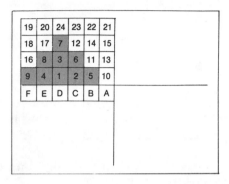

You will notice from the shaded area in this drawing that you are building a sort of pyramid. Study this pyramid. You will quickly see if it is leaning either to the right or left. The adhesive has not set yet so do any straightening necessary before proceeding with tile number 10. Place tile number 10 and proceed until the whole area of that quarter is filled in (with the exception of the border tiles).

E. As you are laying the tiles, press them down firmly and used the rolling pin as added assurance, being careful to keep all tiles square.

F. Using this pattern, complete the other three quarters of the room.

6. Now you are ready to install the border tiles around the circumference of the room.

A. Place a loose tile over a glued tile nearest a border space.

B. Take another loose tile and lay it on top of the loose tile, butting it flush against the wall.

C. Using this butted tile as a guide, draw a line across the other loose tile. This will become the glued-down border tile.

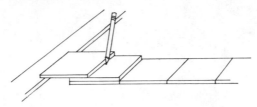

Cut each tile as necessary to complete the border. Do each tile individually as you may not notice if the room is not exactly square.

If there are any pipes to put tile around measure them carefully and cut the tile like this.

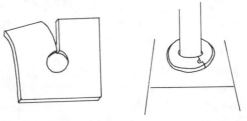

You can buy a special collar from the hardware store which fits around the base of the pipe, giving it a finished look. Give the salesman the diameter of the pipe so that he can supply you with the correct size collar.

If there are any odd shapes to curve the tile around, make a careful pattern of the shape on newspaper, cut

it out and trace around it in the correct position on the tile.

Cut the tile with a sturdy pair of shears or a linoleum knife.

When cleaning up after the job, do *not* use any type of solvent to remove the blobs of paste. Clean up as much as possible as you go along, using a damp cloth. If the adhesive has dried, use a very fine steel wool dipped in water. Rub the spot lightly. If it is very stubborn use some scouring powder. Do not wax the floor for at least three days to give the adhesive a chance to set properly.

To give a finished look to the completed job, consider using the moldings which are available from tile stores. They come in compatible colors and are usually called *vinyl cove bases*.

Designs with tiles.   Don't just lay plain tiles! With very little extra work you can create an attractive, original design on your floor.

First, some hints for using patterned tiles. If you are installing a marblelike tile, you should oppose the direction of the veining of each tile.

If you are using a brick pattern here's a hint.

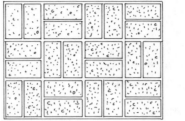

If the bricks are single tiles consider a realistic herringbone effect.

It will take some thinking but if you make a drawing first on graph paper you shouldn't have too much trouble. The important thing is to work slowly and carefully. You don't want to misposition a tile and discover it to your chagrin a week later.

Many varied patterns can be made by combining two colors. You can use colored strips for an effect like this.

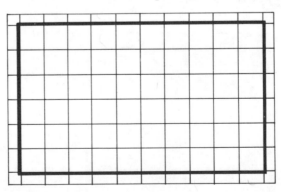

Here are some ideas for basic two-color patterns.

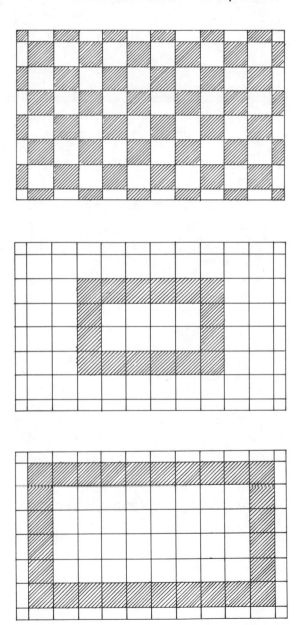

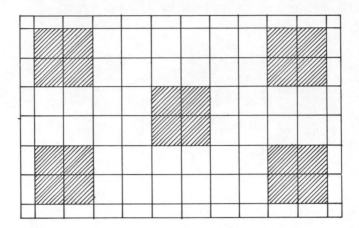

Instead of two colors, consider using solid-color tiles combined with textured or pictorial tiles.

So many combinations can be created. Take graph paper and try to develop your own design. But most of all look. Look at the decorator magazines. Look at dealer displays. Talk to your dealer. He can give you ideas.

Carpet tiles.   One of the "hotter" decorator items to come along recently is the carpet tile. The first ones were of a heavy, feltlike fabric. Now they come with their own adhesive backing, in a variety of colors and patterns and in shag, tufted and matte; some can even be used out-doors. They can be combined very successfully with vinyl tiles, and some companies even put out a matching-pattern tile and carpet combination.

Many people have used kitchen carpet tiles wall-to-wall in their kitchens. If you're concerned about grease stains and spills, the manufacturers claim you needn't be. If that doesn't convince you, the following diagrams show how to combine tile and kitchen carpet for protection against these stains.

Use the same method for laying carpet tiles as for vinyl tiles.

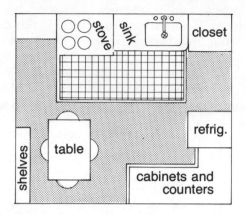

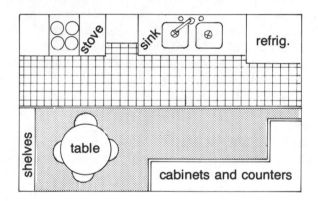

LINOLEUM OR SHEET VINYL

Sheet vinyl (or vinyl plastic) is one of the top-selling resilient floor coverings. However it should be professionally installed. It's not really an easy do-it-yourself item. One advantage of many sheet vinyls is that they may be installed directly over previously laid floors without ripping out the old flooring.

And don't forget about good old-fashioned linoleum (a combination of ground linseed oil and cork.) I know grandma used it and you're new and modern . . . but so is linoleum. The patterns are varied, the colors are deep and true and the slight embossing gives a fairly convincing look. And the price may be quite appealing. Again, laying it is best left to a professional. It's ungainly to handle and awkward to cut. But go to it if your area is small and you think you can handle it. Your dealer can advise you.

REPAIRING A WOOD FLOOR

If all the flooring sags, as it easily could in an older home or apartment, it may be necessary to overhaul it completely. This could mean extra supports in the floor or additional column supports in the basement. It could even mean installing a totally new wood floor. As you can imagine, this is not for you unless you are well advanced in your "do-it-yourselfedness."

On the other hand, some floors can be made sound by simply replacing a few damaged boards, renailing others and refinishing the surface. If a short piece of floorboard is damaged or warped, it's not too difficult to replace.

Usually, finished flooring is called tongue and groove. One floorboard's tongue fits snugly into its neighbor's groove. So go to the lumberyard and ask for tongue and groove of the proper size. It's a good idea to bring a sample of the flooring with you if at all possible. At least bring exact dimensions. Here's how to replace the floorboard.

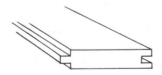

1. With a carpenter's square or ruler, mark off the damaged board which is to be removed.

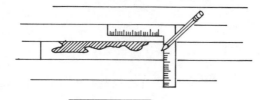

2. Drill a large hole (about ½ inch in diameter) into all four corners of the damaged board. Be care-

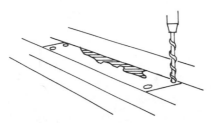

ful to drill only through this finished flooring and not into the wood subflooring beneath.

3. With a wood chisel and hammer, split the damaged piece from one end to the other, along the grain of the wood between the holes.

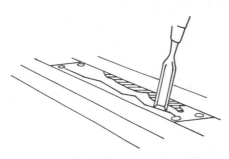

Do this carefully so you won't damage the tongue or groove of the neighboring boards.

4. Cut the correct length of tongue and groove from the piece you have bought at the lumberyard.

5. With the wood chisel, remove the bottom part of the groove from the new piece.

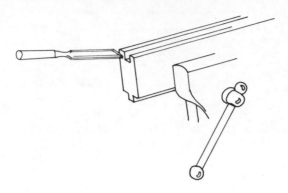

Looked at from one end, your tongue and groove will now look like this.

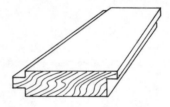

6. Drop the new piece into position, sliding the tongue neatly into its neighbor's groove.

7. Drilling small pilot holes so that the new board won't split, drive in spiral flooring nails at each corner, countersinking them with a nailset or big nail. Then fill the countersunk hole with wood putty or wood plastic.

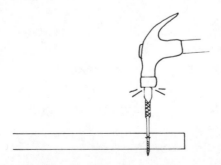

8. If the new piece is lighter in color than the rest of the floor, stain it to match.

If any boards are loose on the floor, drill pilot holes and drive in spiral flooring nails, countersink and fill.

SANDING A WOOD FLOOR

There comes a time in every floor's life when too many muddy feet have tramped over it, too much soot has been ground into it and too many owners have worn a particular path on it. And now you move in. Well, don't move your furniture in yet. Now is the ideal time to rent a couple of sanding machines (one called a drum sander for really grinding off the wax and dirt; the other called a disk sander for doing the edges). You will also need varying grits of sandpaper. The shop where you rent the machines will supply you with sandpaper and will explain how to load the sanders. It's a messy, dusty job, but is well within the realm of your capabilities.

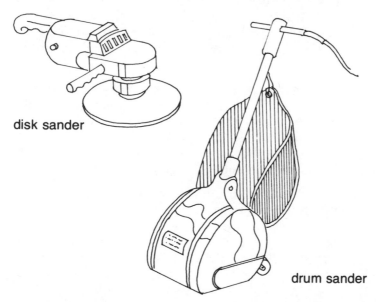

disk sander

drum sander

1. Before starting, nail down and countersink any protruding nails and renail any loose boards with spiral flooring nails.

2. Using the coarsest-grit paper, start the drum sander near one corner. Work backward and forward from wall to wall. Always sand with the grain along the length of the floorboards, *never across*.

3. Never start or stop a sander with the paper in contact with the floor. Those few seconds of standing still will sand a shallow dish into that spot. Tip the sander back before starting it, start slowly rolling it and at the same time lower it onto contact with the floor. Advance along the floor steadily and evenly, being careful not to gouge it by tilting the sander to left or right. When you are a foot or so from the baseboard, still moving, tilt the machine upward, lifting the sandpaper from contact with the floor. Back the machine off, lowering it to contact the floor again and drag the machine backward over the swath you have just cut. Then move on to the next row. Working in this manner, do the whole floor area, avoiding contact with any walls or baseboards (do the edges with the smaller disk sander). Be sure to empty the dust bag each time it's about 30 percent full.

4. Now the major portion of the floor has been rough sanded. Load the smaller edging machine with the same grade coarse paper. Moving the machine in semicircular strokes, sand off the strip left around the edge of the room. Try not to hit into the baseboard molding but edge right up to it.

5. Naturally your circular edging sander won't get into those square corners so this means get down on your hands and knees and rub by hand. Don't be lazy and neglect the corners and behind the pipes. In the end these details count as much as the big areas.

6. After the whole floor has been coarsely sanded, fill the machines with the medium-grit paper. Use the same technique as before. Then, finally, using the fine paper, finish off the job.

7. Vacuum the entire floor thoroughly, picking up every bit of sawdust.

FINISHING THE SANDED FLOOR

Many different finishes can be used on the newly sanded floor. Most of them fall into two general categories: the penetrating floor sealers which do not first need a wood filler, and the finishes which lie on top of the wood like varnish or shellac.

A penetrating floor sealer may be applied with either a cloth or brush. You may want it to be tinted to add a deeper color. This will enhance the natural graining of the raw wood. Follow the instructions for application which are printed on the can.

It is worthwhile to borrow or rent an electric buffer. You can attach a steel wool pad to it to remove any discoloration left on the surface after using the tinted floor sealer. After applying a good floor wax, use the buffer to burnish the waxed surface.

If you plan to use a varnish or shellac on the raw wood, first use a filler product. If a filler is not used, the shellac or varnish will seep into the wood instead of lying on top as it should. Follow instructions on the filler can for application.

Again, talk to your paint dealer. He may suggest a product or technique to use after you tell him your situation.

PAINTING FLOORS

Wooden floors.   Naturally you won't want to apply paint to a fine hardwood floor. It would be better to try to repair or refinish it. However, some floors are not beautiful hardwood. In fact some are plain ugly. So the only alternative may be to paint.

As mentioned in Chapter 10, porch and deck enamels are specifically made to withstand the rigors of the human footfall. These dry to a high gloss and are more effective for wood than either the rubber- or alkyd-based floor enamels. Two thin coats make the floor less susceptible to peeling or blistering than one heavy coat. In fact, it's a good idea to apply the first coat thinned down with turpentine (about six parts paint to one part turpentine). The second coat can be applied straight from the can.

You can also use latex paints which may be thinned with water, though it's not advisable to use them on raw wood or unpainted wood floors. Latex won't take the beating that porch and deck enamel will but it dries to a flat finish and your brushes can be cleaned in water. It can be walked upon after about an hour's drying time. Wait at least until the next day before applying the second coat.

Concrete floors.   For the least problems and effort, your best choice here would be one of the latex floor paints. There is no involved prepainting acid-etch treatment necessary as with many other types of concrete paint. Another advantage of latex is that you can apply resilient floor tiles directly on top of the painted surface without first removing the paint.

To paint any floor, wood or concrete, take the following steps.

1. Wash off all old wax or oil. The salesman at your hardware store will give you a product that includes trisodium phosphate, which is strong enough to cut through many coats of wax.

2. If the old floor is painted and flaky, scrub it down with a wire brush to get rid of all the flakes.

3. Assemble all necessary equipment before starting: rollers, brushes, rags and paint trays.

4. Don'.t paint yourself into a corner!

FLOOR CARE AND MAINTENANCE

Now that you've put such effort into redoing a floor be sure not to ignore your maintenance. Be a good housekeeper!

Wood floors. One of the best ways to insure long life to your floors is to keep them as clean and free of dust and soot as possible. In other words, be a good housekeeper as well as a good handywoman! Use a soft, dry mop or vacuum cleaner.

Give the floors a thorough waxing about four times a year. Never use a self-polishing liquid floor wax on wood! These waxes contain water, and water is the eternal enemy of wood. Use a good brand of paste or cleaning liquid wax (with a *solvent*, not a water base). You should never wash a wood floor with water and soap or water and anything.

Spread the wax evenly over the floor. A fleece applicator simplifies the job and is economical. Rub with the applicator in order to pick up dirt and old wax. Work in sections, using a clean rag, extra wax and elbow grease on stubborn spots.

Let the wax dry the length of time specified on the wax container. Then buff the surface to the luster desired. The more buffing you do, the higher and longer-lasting will be the shine. It might be desirable for you to rent an electric polisher for a small sum. Otherwise buffing is a hard, hands-and-knees job.

If you maintain your wood floors in this way the finish will last forever.

Concrete floors.   Normal cleaning, dusting and washing with soap and water should be all that's necessary to maintain a concrete floor.

However, concrete is quite porous so if the floor is not painted, stains seep in easily. Oil, grease or rust can sometimes be removed by the following method. It's worth a try.

1. Make a wet paste by mixing lemon juice with salt.

2. Put the paste on top of the stain and let it sit for a few minutes.

3. Then scrub with enthusiasm, using a stiff natural-bristle brush. Several applications may be necessary.

If your floor is painted, you may want to apply a coat of wax to it. This will help protect the paint and will give a good-looking surface.

Tile and linoleum.   Sheet vinyl, linoleum and most types of floor tiles—whether they be vinyl, asphalt or rubber—should be washed with a mild soap and warm water. Never use extremely hot water or harsh, abrasive soaps. They can discolor and weaken the durability of the tiles. Rinse off the soap well and mop the floor dry. Allow it to dry thoroughly before applying wax. Use a wax which is recommended by the flooring manufacturer. If this information isn't available, use a self-polishing wax rather than one of the polishing waxes which must be buffed to a luster. Always apply wax in a thin, even coating. Wax put on thickly will not have a proper luster and will not dry adequately. A good self-polishing wax under normal wearing conditions should last for about five weeks.

9. Exciting Walls

Doing anything with walls aside from painting or papering (Chapters 3 and 4) sounds like a monumental task. Don't be intimidated by it. It isn't. Not in this day of precut, matching molding, beautiful prefinished wood panels, corks, and on and on. There are slivers of veneered brick. There are even stones sliced into pieces ready to apply to your walls.

In this chapter I'll go into some of the more popular wall panelings and coverings and tell you how you can do a simple wall in your own home.

CHOOSING WOOD PANELING

Like tile flooring, wall paneling is available with a self-stick adhesive backing. But a note of caution: your present walls must be super-smooth to attach the paneling to them, and the adhesive may not necessarily adhere well to your present painted or papered wall surface. And it may not last the ten or twenty years you want. But if these factors don't disturb you, by all means investigate it. Ask your dealer and if possible describe your present wall surface to him. Complete instructions will be given with the purchase of the panels.

Following are general instructions on how to install regular paneling thoroughly and lastingly.

The first item on the agenda is possibly the most pleasant (aside from the day you step back and admire the wall you yourself have paneled). Go to the lumberyard and choose the color and grain pattern which pleases you. You will see sun-bleached whites, moss greens, silvery grays—all the colors imaginable, some transparent with the wood grain showing through. You will see a full range of natural woods from the lightest birch to the darkest walnut. These panels need the very minimum of care.

Most paneling comes in sheets 4 by 8 feet or 4 by 9 feet. If you can measure accurately, saw carefully and straight and hammer by hitting the nail and not the panel, you should have no difficulty paneling a wall yourself. A power sabre saw will naturally save a lot of time but a good handsaw like the one mentioned in Chapter 1 will do the job.

Suppose you plan to panel a 22-foot-long wall with ceilings 8 feet 4 inches from the floor. Divide the room into 4-foot sections and you will quickly see that you need six 4-by-9-foot panels.

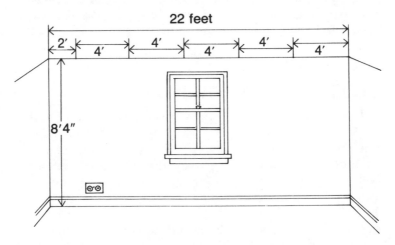

If your wall is more complicated than this, sketch it, inserting measurements, and show it to your dealer. He's an expert and can make size estimates quickly.

YOUR EQUIPMENT

Here are the tools you will need.

1. Good sharp saw

2. Hammer

3. Plumb line (that chalked string with the weight on the end)

4. Carpenter's level

5. Caulking gun (if adhesive is to be used rather than nails)

6. One-inch brads or 1¼-inch finishing nails (or your dealer's recommendation) and 2½-inch common nails for the framing

7. An inexpensive school compass from the five and ten

8. New molding, if needed. (The old molding can be reused if it's in good condition and if you remove it carefully.)

9. One-by-2-inch furring strips (narrow wood strips usually of pine)

10. Nail putty for filling nail holes

11. Carpenter's pry bar or floor chisel for removing moldings

You'll probably have an easier job if you are working on newer construction. An old house has had time to settle itself and walls may not be as square and true as you would like.

PREPARING THE WALL

1. With the pry bar remove all moldings from baseboards, ceilings, doors and windows. If you plan

to reuse the molding, do this job with care. However, if the moldings have been painted and you prefer a wood surface it is easier to buy new molding rather than strip paint off the old. On the other hand, the old moldings are precut to size and mitered and will save some time for that reason. It's up to you to decide. I'll explain how to cut moldings square and how to cut corner miters later in the chapter.

2. Since paneling cannot be nailed directly onto a plaster wall, you must build a framework of 1-by-2-inch furring strips flush against the plaster wall. This framework will be nailed on the wall into the studs behind the plaster. These studs are the vertical construction timbers (two-by-fours) which run from the floor to the ceiling. They are usually placed 16 inches apart, measuring from the center of one two-by-four to the center of the next.

One way to find these studs is to locate nail holes in the base of the wall where the removed baseboard molding has been nailed. If you can spot a nail or nail hole try rapping on the wall above this with your knuckles. If you are on a stud a solid thump will sound as opposed to the hollow thud which sounds in an area a foot away which has no stud. Then it is just a matter of marking off the wall at 16-inch intervals starting at the nail hole.

Another way is to drill small test holes in the wall where you suspect a stud to be located. These holes don't matter as they will eventually be paneled over. This doesn't mean that you should get carried away and act like a woodpecker. You might find your wall all over the floor. Choose a small drill (about $\frac{3}{16}$-inch bit), drill into the wall and if you're still in solid matter after a depth of about $2\frac{1}{4}$ inches remove the drill and see if wood bits come out. If so, you're on a stud. If you only get plaster and a powdering of concrete, or if you get plaster and then space, try another spot.

3. Now nail furring strips into the studs, 16 inches apart horizontally and 48 inches apart vertically (use about a 2½-inch common nail.) You'll avoid mistakes if you mark off the whole wall with pencil guide lines before you start.

When you come to a door or window, completely surround three sides with furring.

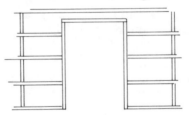

4. If your wall is somewhat uneven, you may need thin shims of wood under low places to level the framing.

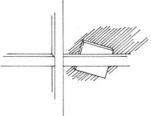

The point is to make this wooden frame of furring as level as possible so that the paneling will not bow or warp when it is nailed or glued onto it. A bowed panel will eventually pull loose because of this constant strain.

INSTALLING PANELS ON THE FURRING FRAME

You will need a helper to complete this job.

As mentioned earlier, plywood paneling usually comes in 4-by-8- or 9-foot sheets. If the panels you have bought have a definite top and bottom, mark the top of each panel on the back with chalk. One misplaced upside down would be difficult to correct. Next lean the panels against the wall to find a pleasing sequence of color or grain pattern. Then number the panels in this order.

Keep in mind that you are going to use both floor and ceiling molding when the panels are up. This will conceal any raggedness at the top and bottom. If you have trouble getting a clean-looking edge at each corner, you can install corner molding. I'll go into this thoroughly later.

1. Start at a corner but beware because most corners are not truly square. This is especially true in older rooms. You cannot butt the panel directly into the corner because if it isn't a true vertical, your whole paneling job will be lopsided. You must custom cut the corner edge of the panel to fit so that the other edge will be a true vertical. Here's how to do it.

A. At a convenient height, measure 50 inches from the corner of the wall and make a mark there. Your measure will be 2 inches wider than the panel.

B. Now make a vertical plumb line, hanging the

chalked string from the ceiling against the wall and snapping it on the wall.

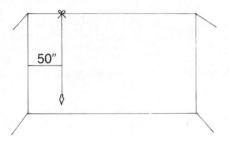

C. Hold the first panel between this chalked line and the corner of the room, lining up one edge flush with the chalked line. Mark the other edge to conform to the corner. An easy and fairly accurate way to do this is to use the school compass.

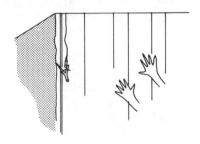

Open it to the width of 2 inches (those 2 inches mentioned in Step A). As your helper is holding the panel in position against the chalk line, run the point leg of the compass down the corner and the pencil leg down the panel. This will automatically inscribe the untrue corner edge onto the panel. Saw or plane along this line to fit the first panel snugly into the corner.

2. Now glue or nail the panels onto the furring-strip frame. Check with your dealer as to which method is best for your walls and room. To nail the panels, use 1-inch brads or 1¼-inch finishing nails.

Nail every 6 inches along the top and bottom and every 12 inches along the sides and horizontal furring.

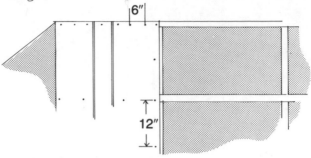

Butt the next panel up against the first. Nail this panel onto the strips of furring. Note that the right edge of the first panel and the left edge of the second panel will be nailed to the same vertical strip of furring. Be sure to keep a good, snug fit and a true vertical as you proceed.

3. Cut around windows as necessary, measuring carefully. Turn off the electricity (see Chapter 6) and remove switch plates and baseboard plug plates. Measure holes in the paneling very carefully so that later you can replace the plates on top of the new panels.

4. Measure your last panel very carefully to accommodate an off-square corner. Transpose the top and then the bottom measure from the wall to the last panel. Cut it to fit.

5. Now countersink all nails (hammer below the surface with a nail set) and fill the resulting holes with a properly colored wood putty.

If after advice from the dealer you decide to glue the panels on, apply the adhesive to the furring strip with a caulking gun. The gun comes with directions for loading it. Press the panel into position and let the adhesive partially set. Then rap the panel firmly into position with a rag-covered block of wood and a hammer. Read the instructions on the adhesive can for more specific instructions regarding the particular adhesive you have chosen.

Now that your wall panels are up you may be disappointed in the appearance of the paneling at the corners. You are an amateur so don't be too upset with yourself. Molding will solve the problem.

Many moldings are available from the dealer who sells the wall paneling. Buy this molding if you can as it is usually color matched to the paneling you have chosen.

For instance, for the corners you can get a finished quarter-round (or shoe) molding which looks like this.

quarter round or shoe

Just nail it onto the first and last panel, snugging it into the corner.

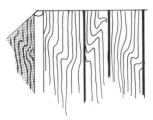

You can also use this molding for the ceiling. Other ceiling moldings are:

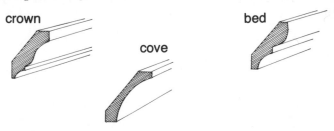

crown

bed

cove

A combination of moldings is often used at the floor. For instance:

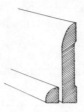

Your main problem with these moldings will be where they meet. You don't want a blunt, cut-off edge where the corner molding meets the baseboard. You will want them to blend into one another. This will require specific types of saw cuts.

Buy a miter box, which is very inexpensive, and a back saw, which costs a little more. Here is how they work.

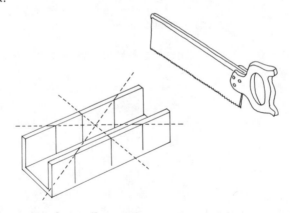

The miter box allows you to cut molding at a 45-degree angle, which allows you to make neat corners like this.

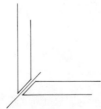

Cutting moldings to the proper 45-degree angle is a bit tricky but if you practice a few times on scrap wood you'll soon be satisfied. One of the secrets is to have your items tightly secure. Be sure the miter box doesn't slip and slide around; if necessary, clamp the molding you are cutting to the miter box.

INSTALLING PANELS ON DRY WALLS

If you have dry walls in your home (masonite, plasterboard, wallboard, etc.) you are in a perfect situation for easy paneling. If the wallboard is level and tight your paneling can be glued directly to it with no concern about making the furring-strip frame needed on plaster walls. Fill the caulking gun with the recommended adhesive and apply it to the panels or walls, using the directions included with the gun and the adhesive.

If you are considering any of the novelty walls like veneer brick, cork or stone, ask your dealer how to proceed. You may not have the proper wall or the task may be beyond your capabilities.

PEGBOARD

Perhaps you have a favorite work area or, lucky you, a whole room for sewing or another hobby—or even your own shop. An ideal wall covering for such an area is pegboard. This is a perforated wallboard which is used with self-locking metal hangers. It is both a space saver and a convenience. It can be installed in the back of a cabinet or a broom closet or exposed to view over the kitchen stove.

These hangers come in quite a variety — hooks for shelves and for hanging just about anything from a heavy vacuum cleaner to a lightweight piece of gay ribbon.

If you install pegboard on a plaster wall you must build

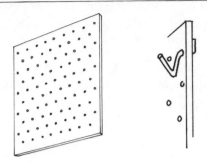

a furring-strip frame (see the section To Prepare the Wall). If the pegboard is to be installed on a dry wall no big problem is involved. Just follow the directions for installing paneling on dry walls.

If you want to hang just a portion of a panel, hang it as you would a bulletin board or picture (see Chapter 2).

CERAMIC TILES FOR WALLS AND FLOORS

If some of the ceramic tiles in your bathroom or kitchen are cracked or broken, replacing them is no great chore. The biggest problem will be to match the color of the tiles, as your present tiles may be old and therefore somewhat faded. However, there are many brands and colors on the market and chances are you'll find a close enough match if you look long enough. Check the yellow pages of the telephone book for tile and plumbing supply dealers. Take a sample of one of your broken tiles (I'll explain how to break one free shortly) and visit these dealers.

Here is a list of the tools you'll need to replace a tile.

1. Cold chisel and hammer to break the cement which holds the tile

2. New cement or adhesive recommended by your dealer

3. Putty knife

4. Masking tape

5. New tile and tile caulking

And now to proceed.

1. With the cold chisel and hammer, break the cement which holds the tile by rapping around the edge or space between tiles. Use care not to break or chip the good tiles which surround the cracked one.

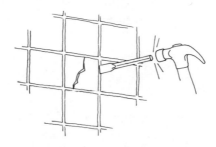

2. Pry behind the tile to loosen it using the cold chisel or, if you feel you need something smaller and narrower, an *old* screwdriver. Again, be careful of those surrounding tiles. Remove the broken tile.

3. Check the fit of the new tile by holding it in the space. If it protrudes, use the cold chisel to chisel away some of the concrete in order to set the new tile into position properly.

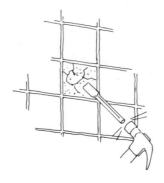

4. I advise using adhesive rather than portland cement as it's easier to handle. Ask your dealer to recommend a brand.

Butter the tile (yes, that's the expression they use) on the back generously with adhesive.

5. Press it quickly into the space—it dries rapidly. Sponge off any excess which squeezes out and align the tile with its neighbors.

6. With masking tape, secure the tile to the wall. Leave this until the adhesive is set. Check it occasionally to be sure it hasn't slipped out of position.

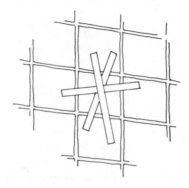

7. When the adhesive is dry, remove the tape. Using the putty knife, press white tile caulking into the cracks around the new tile and smooth it out.

8. Wipe away the excess caulking with water and sponge.

You will notice in your travels around the tiling stores that there is a plastic tile edging available to use as molding. This rounded edging can be used on bathtubs and sinks to give a nice finished look to their edges.

10. Refinishing Furniture

Taking an inexpensive "find" that has been battered and tossed aside and refinishing it into a presentable, proud piece is one of the most satisfying do-it-yourself jobs you will tackle. Chair or cabinet, table or bed, it can be handsomely finished in many ways. Here's how to do it, starting at the beginning.

STRIPPING THE OLD FINISH

If you plan to use opaque paint or an antique, opaque finish and the old surface is good (not checked, blistered or peeling) you will not have to remove this surface. Little preparation beyond washing with disinfectant soap to remove old wax and light sanding to roughen the surface to accept paint will be necessary.

But if the surface is bad or if you plan to use a stain, lacquer or oil, you must remove the old finish. It's a messy job but if all your equipment is handy and you work efficiently it will not be too unpleasant.

Here's what you'll need.

1. Chemical paint remover. If you can buy the liquid remover made strictly for the professional furniture

finisher you will have obtained an effective, inexpensive product. It is usually strong and must be treated with respect as it can burn into skin and ruin fabrics. It is also very flammable so use it with care and, as the fumes are strong, in a well-ventilated area—outdoors if possible. This remover should effectively take off paint, varnish or shellac. The more readily available commercial remover usually found in paint stores is more expensive and less effective. It has been refined to remove some of the strong burning ingredients and is less flammable. Therefore, it might be wiser to get this remover, especially if you must work indoors.

2. Lacquer thinner or paint thinner.

3. A couple of inexpensive *bristle* paintbrushes. *Don't buy nylon or synthetic brushes* as many liquid removers dissolve them. An inexpensive *bristle* nail brush or scrub brush is handy and a couple of old toothbrushes can be put to good use.

4. A putty or broad knife to scrape off the old finish

5. A couple of tin cans (coffee cans are ideal)

6. Medium-coarse steel wool

7. Rubber gloves and very old clothes

Pour the lacquer thinner or paint thinner into one coffee can, filling it about halfway. Fill the other can about halfway with paint remover. If you should get any of the remover on your skin you will feel it burn. Remove it with paint thinner.

1. Spread newspapers well in the area in which you plan to work. The remover will not seep through a couple of layers.

2. Take off any removable hardware (handles, drawer pulls, decorations).

3. Lay on the paint remover with one of the bristle

paintbrushes. Do not paint it on but lay it on in gentle, short brushfuls.

4. Let it sit for about ten minutes. Then with your putty knife push at the surface gently to see if the remover is taking effect. If it is not, wait more time. If it seems loose, lay on a second and heavier application. Let this stand for ten minutes to half an hour, depending upon the thickness of the surface being removed. *Don't try to rush things.*

5. With the edge of the putty knife, scrape in a long, pushing sweep, shoving the old finish off toward the edge.

6. Go over round surfaces like table legs or chair spindles with a scrub brush and scour detailed carving with a toothbrush.

7. You may require another application of the remover. If so, proceed as before. When there is only a small amount of old finish remaining, dip steel wool into the remover and rub in the same direction as the wood grain.

8. When all the old surface has been removed, use lacquer or paint thinner and a scrub brush to take off all the old "gunk." Then rub over the surface with steel wool dipped in thinner, paying attention to stubborn "gunk" stains.

Now you can proceed to apply the type of finish you prefer.

STAINING

Staining means applying a somewhat darker, transparent dye which enhances the color and wood grain of the item being treated.

1. Sand the piece, starting with a medium paper,

working your way up to an extra-fine paper and ending with fine steel wool. Sand and sand with the

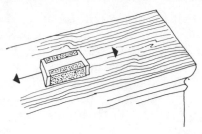

grain until your arm is ready to fall off, then use steel wool until it does. Try to get rid of every flaw. This is critical, as the succeeding operations depend upon the thoroughness of this one. If there is a gouge or chip too deep to remove by sanding, fill the gap with wood putty. Check with your dealer. He will help you select an appropriate filler or putty. As an alternative save some of the fine sawdust from your sanding, mix it with white wood glue and use this as your filler. When it has dried, sand it smooth to match the surrounding surface. Be sure to clean off all sanding dust, using a vacuum cleaner if necessary.

2. Before applying the stain it is wise to apply a filler or sealer. This insures that the stain will apply evenly and won't soak in dark and blotchy where the wood is very porous. This is essential when using soft, grainy woods like pine, fir or mahogany. An effective sealer is four parts denatured alcohol to one part shellac. After this is thoroughly soaked in and dry (about twenty-four hours), steel wool the piece again. Clean off the steel-wool filings.

3. A ready-mixed oil-base stain gives good, professional-looking results. There are about as many refinishing theories as there are amateur refinishers. Some swear that the only stain worth anything is one which you have mixed yourself, but I feel that the commercial "ready" mix is a fine product.

Go to the paint supply store and ask for an oil-stain color chart. These charts often show a color swatch of the particular stain as applied to pine and then applied to its corresponding wood.

Example: Walnut on pine
Walnut on walnut

If you're working with inexpensive, unfinished raw furniture you can be fairly well assured that it is the wood of an evergreen (pine, fir). These stain in a fairly similar fashion.

You can identify other raw woods by their texture and color.

REDDISH WOODS   = Mahogany, cherry or rosewood
YELLOW WOODS   = Pine, birch, golden oak, fir
BROWN WOODS   = Walnut, dark oak, "fruitwood"
ORANGE WOODS   = Maple, cedar

If you attempt to do something exotic like applying walnut stain on mahogany wood, don't expect to get the color shown on the color chart. Your best bet is to try a sample spot in an out-of-sight area of the furniture to be sure that your combination works well.

Following the instructions on the can of oil stain, apply the stain to the furniture. After the allotted time, wipe it off with a clean, absorbent rag (not nylon or silk). *Don't* apply the stain and forget to wipe it off for an hour or so. You'll have a blotchy, uneven mess.

APPLYING THE FINISH

Varnish.   After the staining operation, let the job stand for twenty-four hours. Then mix one part varnish with four to five parts paint thinner in a can (a coffee can with a tight plastic lid is perfect). Apply this to the piece with a soft paint brush, brushing it in well and leaving no puddles or drips. Let it sit overnight until it's thoroughly dry.

With fine steel wool firmly buff the piece in the direction of the grain. You will see a slight luster beginning. Brush away the steel wool dust and apply a second coat of the varnish/paint thinner. Again, wait overnight until it's dry and buff with steel wool. Do this combination of applying the liquid and buffing with steel wool about four times. By the time you're through (five days later) you'll have a lustrous satin finish.

As a final touch, rub in a clear paste wax like butcher's wax. Rub it with a clean cloth and buff it with another clean cloth. (A man's T-shirt is a perfect final buffer if you can sweet-talk one from your favorite man.)

If you should desire a high-gloss finish for the piece, go through all the steps mentioned but on the final application of varnish/paint thinner, use one part varnish and one part thinner. Do not follow through with the steel wool. Upon this final application, try to avoid any activity that might stir up dust which would settle on the surface.

This operation gives a lovely though not too durable finish. Be sure everyone has a coaster. If you're doing a bar or breakfast table which gets a lot of rough use, I recommend the polyurethane finish mentioned further on in this section.

Shellac. After the staining operation, let the job stand for twenty-four hours. Then mix one part shellac with five parts denatured alcohol. Apply this to the piece with a soft paint brush. When this has dried (overnight) buff it with fine steel wool and apply another coat of the shellac/alcohol combination. Again, steel wool the piece. Do this five or six times and you will have a handsome satin finish.

Though not mentioned often by professionals because of its lack of durability, this is one of my favorite and most successful finishes.

Polyurethane finishes. These plastic finishes are tough and durable. They are excellent when used on bar tops, kitchen tables and work tables. Take your choice of high gloss, satin finish (medium gloss) or flat finish.

When proceeding, follow the very complete instructions on the can to the letter.

HAND-RUBBED OIL FINISH

Admittedly, a handsome piece results from the hand-rubbed finish but a great amount of hard work goes into the job. If you are working with a high-quality, beautifully grained wood, it can be worth the effort.

1. Combine two parts fast-drying varnish and one part polymerized (boiled) linseed oil to three parts paint thinner. The plastic-lidded coffee can is ideal for this.

2. Work this formula into the wood using a soft rag, your bare hands or, best of all, wearing old kid or leather gloves. Apply it with the ball of your hand until it no longer will soak into the wood. Then the wood will have had enough. Your hand is one of the best tools here.

3. After this has soaked in well (about an hour) wipe the surface with a clean rag. If there is tackiness, dip the rag into paint thinner and rub until it has no tack. Let this sit to dry overnight.

4. If there is any unevenness the next day it means that part of the wood has not been thoroughly saturated. Go to work on these portions with oil and wipe them after an hour. Again let dry overnight.

5. Apply a second and if necessary a third coat of the formula, rubbing it down and letting it dry overnight. It should now have an even, all-over finish.

6. As a finish coat, apply the formula and do *not* let it stand for an hour. Rub it down with a flannel pad until there is no tackiness left.

This finish, as you can conclude, becomes part of the wood and does not lay on top. It is durable and beautiful.

PAINTING WITH ENAMEL

One convenient thing about working with enamel is that it can be its own primer and sealer, though you may have to apply a few coats. Unless the item to be painted has many knots, enamel may be applied directly onto raw wood. If there are knots, they should be painted first with one part shellac and one part denatured alcohol. Otherwise, no matter how many coats of paint are applied, the knots will bleed through.

Be sure to remove all possible hardware and decorations. Fill any gouges or knot holes with wood putty and sand when the putty has dried.

Don't be fooled into believing that painting covers a multitude of sins. Careless sanding or unfilled holes show up just as glaringly as with a stained finish. If the item has an old finish, wash it down with strong detergent to cut the dirt and wax. Then sand it to rough it up so that the enamel will adhere properly. Clean up the sand dust.

If the piece has been previously painted and is in good condition except for a few chips and nicks, sand these flush with the surrounding area. Lightly sand the whole item to roughen it up. If the piece has many old coats of paint on it so that the details of the piece are blurred (carvings and spindles indistinct) or if the old paint is peely and bad you'd better remove the old finish as described in the beginning of this chapter. Then paint as follows:

1. Buy a good brand of quick-drying enamel. Don't try to scrimp by looking for a bargain, as you may wait two or three days for drying and then get poor coverage as your penny-saving reward. Note that the enamel will specify indoor, outdoor or indoor/

outdoor. (For the uses of various outdoor enamels see the section Outdoor Furniture in this chapter.)

2. After laying newspapers around the item to be painted, pry open the enamel can with a screwdriver. Mix the paint thoroughly.

3. Lay the first coat of enamel on the item, brushing it in fairly well. Dip the brush in so that the bristles are halfway covered with paint. Dipping too deep will result in a lot of runs and drips. If the wood is raw the enamel will probably soak in. When it has dried, sand the item lightly but thoroughly. Clean up the sand dust.

4. Lay the second coat on, stroking it on fairly heavily in the shorter direction and smoothing it out in long, gentle strokes in the long direction.

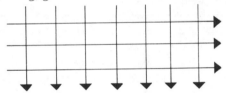

5. Two coats should adequately cover the item but if you feel you need a third coat, lightly sand the second coat after it has dried. Then apply the third coat.

One of the advantages of using a quick-drying enamel is that there is less time for dust to settle upon the item and mar its surface. Try to work in an area where dust is not stirred up by activity.

Children's furniture.   If you have children who are at the gnawing age, ask your dealer about enamels for the crib, highchair, playpen and other funiture. Lead-free paints are available that cause no harm or illness when chewed upon. In fact, if you plan any major redecorating when you have small children, it would be a good idea to use lead-free paint throughout the house.

ANTIQUE AND GLAZED FINISHES

This is really the lazy woman's way (and I don't say this disparagingly) to get a pleasing finish on an old or unpainted piece. Unless the piece is in bad shape, the old finish does not have to be removed. Antiquing can cover a multitude of sins. As the purpose is to make the item look antique, holes and dents look less like accidents.

Antique finishes consist of a colored base coat and a translucent "glaze" color which is rubbed on top of the base coat to give the piece a two-color effect. Usually the top glaze is similar in color to many oil stains. Many manufacturers have produced kits with all the necessary ingredients enclosed. Go to your dealer, look around at swatches and samples and decide from there.

Here is how to use these kits.

1. Prepare the piece for painting by removing the hardware, washing away old wax and dirt, filling in holes with wood putty and sanding the item. If you are working on raw wood with no old finish on it, it would be advisable to use a primer-sealer paint before proceeding.

2. If you have bought a kit, one can will contain flat finish paint in the color you have chosen. The other can is your glaze. Apply the paint, being careful to avoid drips and runs.

3. When dry, sand the piece and if necessary apply a second coat of flat paint. Clean up the sandings.

4. Let the piece stand for three or four days before applying the glaze. This will give the paint time not only to dry but to harden completely.

5. After stirring the can of glaze well, brush it onto the piece sparingly.

6. Usually the kit comes supplied with cheesecloth.

Scrunch it up (do not be neat and fold it) and wipe most of the glaze off. On the high edges of a turned spindle or on the center area of a flat piece, rub more off to give a highlighted look. As you blend toward the edges the glaze tone should be deeper. You may want to leave heavier glaze in indented, carved areas to emphasize the carving. It's a good idea to practice on scrap material and experiment with effects.

OUTDOOR ENAMELS AND FINISHES

Treat wooden outdoor furniture in the same manner as any other furniture needing paint. Wash it clean, sand it where needed and then use *outdoor* enamel on it.

If you are painting outdoor steps or stairs of wood or a porch deck, use regular marine deck paint. That's the real tough stuff which will withstand water and a lot of hard walking and scuffing.

If your outdoor furniture is of natural wood, use marine or spar varnish. This also will withstand any spring, summer and autumn weather.

If rust spots show on painted metal furniture, use steel wool, rubbing until the spot shows shiny. Then paint these areas with rust-resistant paint before you apply the outdoor enamel.

No painting or varnishing is necessary on tubular aluminum furniture. The only maintenance necessary to prevent pitting is a light coat of paste wax. Rub it on and wipe it with a clean rag. If the furniture has already become pitted, rub it down with steel wool and then wax.

Redwood, according to the salesman, needs absolutely no care. But your picnic table and lounge chair will look better and last longer if you coat them each year with a redwood sealer. Food stains won't sink in and that nice red color will be maintained. Paint all surfaces including the undersides. Pay special attention to the legs, which very often must sit in dampness or rain puddles.

Rattan furniture is very pretty and popular but a curse to paint with a brush. Here's where the aerosol spray can saves you time. You can buy either outdoor spar varnish or enamel or a plastic spray coating. This type of furniture, cast-iron scrolls, curlicues or any other intricate patterns lend themselves perfectly to spraying. But be forewarned that a couple of wicker chairs will gobble up a lot of spray cans.

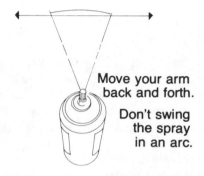

Move your arm back and forth.

Don't swing the spray in an arc.

If you've ever tried to paint a wrought-iron railing with a brush or spray can, you know how frustrating it is. Now you can buy a fuzzy terrycloth mitten which you wear. Dip it into the paint, squeeze it out by making a fist and rub it onto the rails and curlicues.

11. Furniture Repair

Do you have a table with a wobbly leg, or a chair that gives your guests a terrible pinch, or a perfectly good bed with the top of one bedpost broken off, or a thousand other furniture ills which add more irritations to an already annoyance-plagued day? Cheer up! You can very easily get rid of these bothers. Not by throwing the furniture out but by fixing it.

This chapter will cover simple basic repairs starting alphabetically with "beds" and ending with "veneer."

BEDS

If you closely examine the following style bed, you will see that it has a wooden framework of two sides which lock into a headboard and footboard. Removable bed slats keep the box spring from falling through to the floor.

If the bed slats fall out, they are too short. Perhaps the bed is old and the frame has warped.

1. Be sure the frame fits together securely and that the lip on which the slats rest is securely fastened to the side boards.

2. If the frame and lip are secure, go to the lumber-

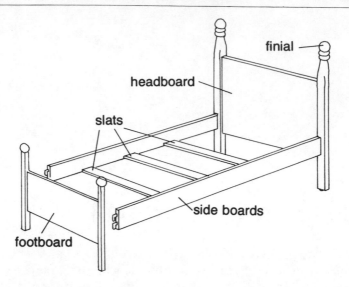

yard and ask for the necessary length of "bed slat." Yes, that's what it's called.

3. Measure the space for the slat and cut the slat ¼ inch smaller than the space. Cut cleanly and squarely. (The miter box may be helpful here. See the explanation of miter boxes in Chapter 9.)

Sometimes, instead of a wooden frame, your box spring will rest on an iron frame to which the headboard and footboard are attached. Be sure all the nuts and bolts on the frame are tight. No slats are necessary here as the iron frame is built to accommodate the box spring.

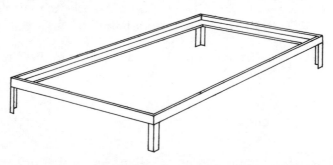

If the ornamental top (finial) on a wooden headboard or footboard has broken off it can sometimes be fixed. If this top is part of the whole bedpost like this you're out of luck. Take the repair to a professional.

But if the top ornament has been separately doweled onto the rest of the post like this and the top has broken off at the dowel,

1. Cut the dowel off.

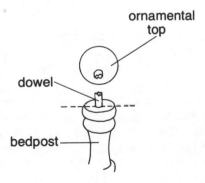

2. Buy a dowel stick (about ten cents at the hardware store) of a similar size to the broken one.

3. Choosing a drill bit to match the new dowel, drill a hole in the ornamental top and another in the bed post itself. Be sure to drill as squarely as you can.

4. Cut the new dowel stick to a proper length to fit the drilled holes, apply glue to it and tap into the post. Rap the ornamental top onto it.

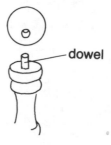

Don't rap the ornament itself with a hammer. You may damage it. Hold scrap wood on top of the ornament and hammer on the scrap.

If this same top ornament (finial) has split beyond repair, you can replace it with a new one. Fancy tops for banisters or gate posts can be bought from many hardware or lumber stores or through one of the large mail-order catalogs. Usually these tops come unfinished. If you have trouble matching the wood on the post accurately, this might be an ideal situation to try one of the new antiquing kits or a bright enamel (see Chapter 10) to give the whole bed a fresh look.

CASTERS

It's frustrating to try to move a very portable piece, only to find that the casters are loose or that they just won't roll.

Take a close look at the balky caster. Perhaps lint or a piece of thread has become wrapped around the wheel or axle. Cut this thread away. Give the moving parts a drink of household oil while working the caster back and forth and the wheel part around and around. Don't drown it in oil! Just a drop will do.

If the casters are loose, check that the screws are tight. If one of the screws turns around and around uselessly without tightening up, remove the screw, put plastic wood into the hole, let it harden and rescrew in the screw.

Some casters have a shank which fits into a socket. If this is loose, remove the caster from the socket, wrap the shank with masking or electrical tape and reinsert it into the socket.

CHAIRS

Mending and brightening outdoor chairs.   Don't throw away that shabby wooden deck chair with the torn canvas. A coat of enamel on the frame and some gaily striped canvas or plastic will make it look pretty close to new.

1. Remove the old, torn canvas. Save it to use as a pattern for the new.

2. Remove all old tacks from the wood frame.

3. Buy new canvas. You may be able to find the exact width. If not, use your old canvas as a pattern. Cut to size, fold the edges under and stitch them for extra strength.

4. Double the material where it is to be tacked onto

the wood frame. Use copper tacks, spacing them about 1½ to 2 inches apart—or use your heavy-duty staple gun instead.

If your aluminum chair is in sad shape, you can buy strips of plastic webbing in kit form. Attach this webbing to the aluminum chair with the special fasteners which many manufacturers provide in the webbing kit or with sheet-metal screws. Fasten the special fasteners according to the directions and weave the plastic strips again as directed on the package.

If your folding chair has become stiff with age, remove the old grime from the folding joints and treat them to a squirt of oil.

Protect your chairs to give them a longer life. If possible, put them away at night and shield them from those soaking summer storms. Store them away in the winter, and in the spring get them out of hibernation with soap, water and a new oiling.

Fixing indoor wooden chairs.   If any of the joints are loose or keep coming out—an arm, back, seat or leg—sand off the old glue, reglue with a good wood glue (white glue or a plastic resin glue) and keep the joint under pressure until the glue is dry. This is best done by tying the injured item with strong cord and a tourniquet.

Here are some examples. The cord is tied around the item, the scrap of wood is twisted with the cord to tighten the cord and then the wood is slipped under one of the chair's rungs to keep it from spinning untwisted.

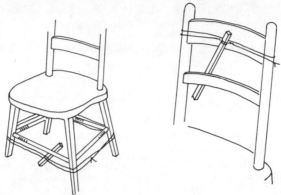

When the rung of a chair keeps coming loose, even after repeated gluing, there are a couple of tricks you can use.

1. For a temporary repair, wrap the end with thread before regluing and inserting the rung.

2. Or, after you have glued and inserted the rung, glue toothpicks and tap them into and around the rung. When they're dry, cut them off as short as possible.

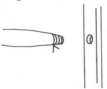

3. For a more professional repair, make a short cut on the end of the rung with a saw and insert a small wooden wedge. This wedge will expand the rung for a snug fit. Apply glue and insert the wedged rung into the hole. (Here's a hint. The end of a clothespin is a ready-made wedge.)

Hold the rung in place with strong cord until the glue dries. If a simple gluing doesn't remedy the wobbly frame, you can apply extra support on the underside.

1. Measure the size needed and buy metal angle irons.

2. Making a pilot hole with your threaded awl, position these irons as illustrated.

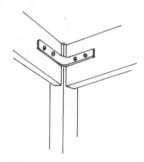

3. Or, with a miter box, cut a wedge which looks like this, using a 45-degree angle. Drill two small holes in the wedge. Cut four wedges, one for each corner.

4. Place the four wedges as shown on the underside of the chair and screw through the wedges and into the chair.

If the leg, rung or rail of a chair has split with the grain of the wood, use a good wood glue to glue the two halves together, following the directions on the glue container. Using a C-clamp, clamp the two portions together. Wipe off any excess glue which squeezes out. Let the piece dry for twenty-four hours.

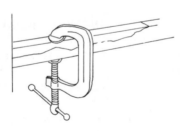

If the wood curves and it is awkward to place a C-clamp in position, tie the piece together with strong string.

Now for that wooden seat which pinches your friends so unceremoniously.

1. Force open the crack and glue along both its

sides. Tie the seat together with string until the glue is dry.

2. Buy metal mending plates which look like this. Two should be sufficient.

Be sure to buy the four-hole kind. Turn the chair over and put these into position on the wooden seat as illustrated. Make pilot holes with the threaded awl and screw the plates into position.

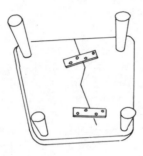

Upholstered chairs.   Reupholstering furniture is a job well left to the professional upholsterer or expert needle-woman. If you'd like to learn there are many excellent books on the subject.

However, there are certain simple repairs that can be made by a novice. For instance, if the chair is made of wood but has a removable upholstered seat (many bridge chairs are like this) it's simple to replace the covering.

1. Turn the chair upside down and remove the four screws holding the seat in position onto the chair frame.

2. Buy new material, perhaps a rich-looking leath-erette or a bright upholstery fabric.

3. Remove the old material from the chair seat (it is

usually stapled or tacked on). Save this to use as a pattern for the new fabric.

4. Cut out the new fabric, using the old as a pattern. If the cushioning in the seat is lumpy and old, replace it with a piece of foam rubber, which you can buy at an upholstery shop.

5. Wrap the new fabric tightly over the cushioned part of the chair and secure the four sides with tacks or staples. You may want to fold a hem in the material where the tacks go, for extra strength.

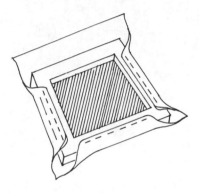

6. Tuck in the corners as illustrated and tack or staple all around the seat.

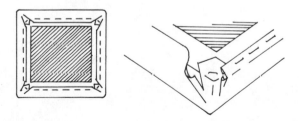

If the seat of an overstuffed chair sags, tip the chair upside down.

1. Remove the dust cover which hides the webbing and springs. Then remove the old webbing.

2. With strong string and tacks, tie the bottom of each spring coil to the one next to it and to the frame (see illustration for grid of string and tying points).

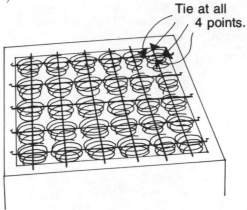

3. Buy new webbing and replace it using ¾-inch tacks. Double the webbing over before hammering in the tacks to insure strength. Weave the webbing so that each spring rests squarely on the crossing of the woven strip.

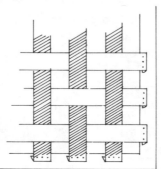

4. Pull the webbing as taut as possible before tacking it onto the frame.

A. Use a webbing stretcher or double the end of the webbing around a board. Jam the board against the chair frame and bend it downward.

Tack the webbing with one tack just to hold it for now. This stretching is vital if you want your webbing job to last more than a month!

B. Cut the webbing, leaving from 1¾ to 2 inches beyond the tack. Fold this excess back to rest on top of the frame and nail in three or four tacks. Trim off the extra webbing as close as possible.

5. To insure that the springs stay in position, sew each spring directly to the webbing with heavy-duty thread.

6. Replace the old dust cover. If it's shabby, buy new material. Cut it using the old dust cover as a pattern, hem the raw edges and attach the cover with staples or tacks.

Now your chair is trussed up like a turkey at Thanksgiving, ready for anything, even heavy Uncle Freddy.

Rush- or cane-seated chairs.   Rushing or caning a chair comes under the heading of "professional." Although a nonprofessional can attempt it, it requires dexterity, skill and patience.

However, if there is a small hole in your caned chair a patch can be faked onto it. Don't expect your matched-up piece to be perfect. It will be noticeable at more than a glance.

1. Order matching cane from a mail-order house or a shop. (See your telephone yellow pages or ask your lumberyard, hardware store or furniture store —all of whom are probably getting to know you well at this point.)

2. Soak the cane in warm water until it's pliable.

3. Trim off any broken ends on the underside of the seat as close as possible.

4. Matching the weave as well as possible, weave in the new cane, tucking the ends under the old cane to conceal them.

5. Glue these ends in place with wood glue. Then cover them with wax paper and clamp them either by putting weight on the cane or by putting boards on both sides and tying them together with cord. (The wax paper is a good trick to keep glue from sticking where you don't want it to stick.)

Wicker or rattan chairs.   Usually a wicker or rattan chair has strips of the reed bound around and around the rungs and often the arms. Occasionally these become dry and brittle, break and start to unwind themselves.

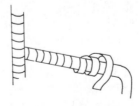

1. Remove the old binding, cutting it off at the

point where it is still securely attached to the chair. Cut it off at the underside or in the least noticeable place.

2. Buy a new strip of wicker binding and soak it in water until it is pliable.

3. Apply wood glue to the chair rung, attach one end of the strip with a short, thin brad and wrap the remainder around the glue-coated rung.

4. Secure the other end with another brad.

If a densely woven area of wicker is split or has a hole, you can weave in a patch.

1. Soak the new wicker to make it pliable.

2. Towel dry it, and on the underside glue the new strip onto one of the old ones. For added strength you can also wire the two pieces together. Poke a pin through both pieces to make a hole, draw thin wire through the two holes and twist it together underneath.

3. Follow the weave as best you can. Reweave the hole as you would darn a hole in a sock. Then attach the end of the strip to one of the old strips as you attached the beginning.

DRAWERS

The most common problem with furniture drawers is that they're apt to stick. In fact, they can stick so stubbornly that the strength of an Atlas won't open them. This is especially so in the hot, damp days of summer.

1. Open the drawer as far as you can and rub the edges with paraffin or one of the new silicone lubricants. Slide the drawer in and out to drag the paraffin into as much of the swollen areas as possible.

2. If you can get the drawer open wide enough, slide in a lighted bulb which is protected by a wire cage. Leaving it for a couple of hours with the drawer open should shrink the swollen wood enough to get the drawer out.

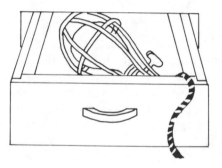

3. After the drawer is out, look for the points where the rubbing occurs. These points will often show up as darker, shiny streaks along the sides or edges. Sand down these high spots with a piece of medium sandpaper wrapped around a block of wood.

4. If the drawer is subject to a lot of dampness and will only swell again, paint all surfaces of the drawer (except of course the front face, which shows) with varnish or shellac. After this is thoroughly dry, coat the sliding edges with paraffin or silicone lubricant.

If the joints of the drawers are loose, take the loose joint apart, scrape off the old glue, reglue and tie the drawer with a tourniquet and strong cord.

If the bottom of the drawer is loose, remove it and scrape away all the old glue. Most drawer bottoms rest neatly in a routed-out groove in the drawer sides. This groove is called a rabbet. Replace the glue in this rabbet and set the drawer bottom into it. To be sure the bottom will hold firmly, nail in a couple of small, thin brads.

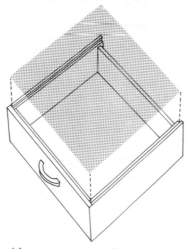

(drawer now upside down)

If the drawer bottom is cracked you can easily replace it with a piece of hardboard or ⅛-inch plywood. Just measure carefully and cut on your measure with a saw.

Drawer pulls and knobs.   Sometimes you can spark up a drab, old piece that you're tired of just by changing the hardware. White porcelain knobs can replace the old, finger-marked wooden ones. Or the old-fashioned metal ones can be replaced by contemporary brass. Look around your local stores or check the large mail-order catalogs to see what's available.

If a drawer pull is loose and nothing happens when you try to tighten the screw holding it, the hole which the screw is in has become enlarged with wear and age. Fill the hole with plastic wood, let it dry and start a new hole on top of the plastic wood with the threaded awl. Insert the wood screw into this pilot hole and reset the screw.

If you plan to put hardware on a piece (perhaps an unpainted piece) where no holes have been bored, be sure to start with a small pilot hole. This helps prevent splitting and splintering. When you are about to come through the back side, drill gently to prevent splintering.

TABLES

Many of the same ailments plaguing chairs apply also to tables. So you can repair table legs and rungs in the same way as you would chair legs and rungs.

If the table's leg is loose, try to force additional glue into the joint or, better still, try to pull the leg away from the joint, scrape away the old glue, apply new glue and tie it in place using a tourniquet.

If neither of these solves the problem:

1. Cut the corner off a 1- to 1¼-inch-thick board.

2. Measure the underside of the table's leg and then, using a miter box, notch out a 90-degree corner.

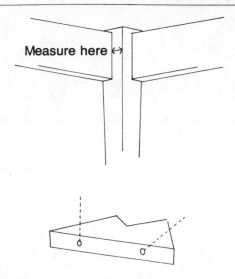

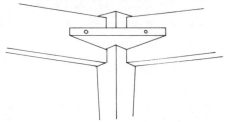

3. Drill pilot holes and, using wood screws, screw this corner onto the table frame as shown. Be sure not to use screws which are too long and will come through on the front face.

Screw notched block to frame.

Table-top joints separated.   If the boards that make up a table top have become separated follow these steps

1. Remove the top from the frame and legs.

2. Scrape away all the old glue.

3. Apply new glue and press the boards together.

4. If you have the web-type furniture clamps, use them. If not, tie the table top with strong cord at three or four points. Tie it tightly but not so much that the boards curve. Be sure the table top stays flat.

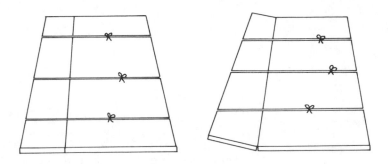

REPAIRING WOOD SURFACES

Small scratches and chips.   The best way to repair scratches and chips is to apply matching stain. You can buy a small bottle at your paint dealer. Follow the instructions on the bottle. Apply the stain carefully, covering only the scratch and not the undamaged surrounding area.

Then when the stain has thoroughly dried, just as carefully apply a coat of varnish to the scratch. Apply a second coat the next day.

An alternative method is to use a stick of wax resembling a child's crayon, which· can be bought in a very close color match. Just crayon over the scratch.

There are many temporary repairs you can make using items you probably have around the house, but these remedies are far from satisfactory. However, if you suddenly can't live with those scratches and the gang is about to arrive for Thanksgiving dinner, here's a quick guide to temporary remedies.

For walnut or fruitwood: the meat of a walnut rubbed into the scratch, or brown shoe polish

Ebony: black shoe polish

Maple or mahogany: iodine

Stains.   *Water and alcohol stains* can often be removed from a lacquered, varnished or shellacked surface.

1. Rub the stain first with cigarette ashes made into a paste by mixing with castor oil.

2. If this fails, put spirits of camphor on a rag and daub it on the stain. Let this dry for about forty-five minutes. With a cloth dipped in machine oil, rub rottenstone (available from your hardware store) on the stain. Rub in the same direction as the grain of the wood. This will probably remove a lot of the finish and you may have to restain the surface. If refinishing is not necessary, use paste wax and elbow grease.

Heat stains are more difficult to contend with.

1. First rub the stain with spirits of camphor or camphorated oil. Polish it with a soft cloth.

2. If this doesn't succeed, use a cloth soaked in oil and rubbed with rottenstone. But again, you may have to refinish the surface.

A *wet newspaper* has been delivered in a rainstorm and you've carelessly thrown it on the dining table. Late that evening you pick up the paper and half of it adheres like glue to the table. Soak the paper with olive oil. Let it sit for ten minutes and then rub it off with a clean cloth.

Candle wax is best removed by taking off as much as you can with your fingers. Then scrape off the remainder with a dull butter spreader or table knife. Wipe what's left with a clean cloth dipped in benzine.

Dents which are shallow or have been made with a blunt instrument can often be remedied. Try to do this without removing the finish. If the following steps are unsuccessful, remove the finish and apply each step again.

1. Apply a damp cloth to the area for several hours. Do not let the cloth dry out. Keep it damp. This should swell the wood fibers.

2. Then apply a warm iron over the damp cloth. This should draw the dent upward toward the heat.

Burns of a minor nature can be helped. If the burn is only on the top surface and has left a yellowish-brown stain, apply paste silver polish. After removing the polish, apply paste wax.

A more serious burn takes more effort. If a careless guest has left a cigarette on the table and it has slightly charred the top, scrape out the charred wood with a sharp knife. Do this carefully as you don't want to gouge out any good wood. Scrape with the grain of the wood. Clean the scar with benzine, burnish with fine steel wool and apply an oil stain of the proper color.

If in removing the charred wood you leave a noticeable pit, fill this pit with stick shellac, following the directions on the stick. After the shellac has set, lightly rub the filled pit with fine steel wool and then with paste wax.

Veneer.   Many pieces of furniture are made of an inexpensive wood and then covered with a thin skin of fine wood. This thin sheet of wood is called veneer.

Through age, heat or damp this veneer can pull loose from the furniture.

Here's how to repair it.

1. Carefully bend the veneer away from the furniture. Avoid breaking the veneer. Scrape away as much of the old glue as possible.

2. Apply new glue. Wipe away any which oozes out from the edges and clamp the piece. If a clamp can't be used—on a table top or side of a chest, for example—tape the repair with tautly applied masking tape. Or plunk that big, heavy, well-read volume of Shakespeare's complete works onto the table top and use it as a weight. Be sure to put a rag underneath in case glue oozes out.

The next procedure is a bit tricky but it's worth a try if the veneer is blistered.

1. Slit the blister with a razor blade in the same direction as the grain of the wood.

2. With the flat of the blade of a knife, carefully lift the slit edges of the veneer.

3. With a toothpick dipped in wood glue, spread the glue on the underside of the split. Press the edges together. If the blister was large and the edges now overlap, trim a sliver off one edge with the razor blade.

4. Wipe away any excess glue and weight the repaired blister down until the glue is dry.

If the veneer is missing or broken the repair is even trickier. But if you have the patience, give it a try.

1. Cut out the broken or missing section in a careful square or rectangular shape. This can be done with a very sharp knife or razor blade.

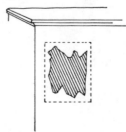

2. Scrape away all the old glue possible.

3. Buy a new sheet of veneer. If you can, take a sliver of the broken section with you to match it with the new veneer.

4. Carefully cut the new veneer to match the area to be patched. Experiment first to see which tool you handle best: razor blade, sharp knife or (not really recommended) scissors.

5. Glue the cut piece into position (be sure the grain is going in the right direction) and hold it in place with weights, tape or clamps until the glue is dry. You can see now how critical it is to do all the cutting carefully so that as perfect a match as possible can be made.

6. The new piece probably needs refinishing, as new veneer is usually raw wood. Sand it with fine sandpaper, apply a matching stain and refinish (see Chapter 10).

12. Household Pests

As much as you scour and scrub, as much as you polish and shine, you can still be plagued by pests.

Don't get me wrong! Polishing and scrubbing does help to be rid of them.

FABRIC-EATING INSECTS

Moths. Here you see a drawing of a moth and the grub from which the moth comes. The grub (larva) is yel-

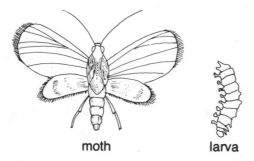

moth   larva

lowish-brown or brown and is about ½ inch long. It is this grub which is the fabric eater. Grubs feed on fabrics which are of vegetable or animal origin. This means your fur coat, your feather boa, wools, cottons, linens and silks, just to mention a few. These hearty eaters leave the synthetics like nylon and orlon strictly alone.

The best way to control these pests is to:

1. Keep clothing, blankets and rugs clean, and also keep their storage areas clean.

2. Store clothing, blankets and drapes in a closet or chest with naphthalene flakes or balls.

3. If the pests are already there, surface spray the affected areas with methoxychlor or perthane.

Carpet beetles.   The adult beetles are outdoor insects which lay their eggs on feathers or in hair. A favorite hatching place is in birds' nests or on your dog's back. After the small, hairy larva pictured here hatches, it eats

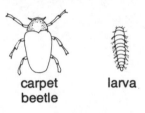

carpet   larva
beetle

its way through all sorts of clothing, saving woolens for the main course.

To help control these pests:

1. Search out any old nests around your house. Take a good look at your favorite pet after a day in the country.

2. Use moth repellent to discourage these creatures.

3. And again, cleanliness counts.

Book lice.   These miniature creatures resemble scurrying bits of dust. They devour damp, moldy books which are stored in the attic or basement for long periods. Rather than the paper, their tasty repast is the glue used

book louse

in book binding—in getting to this glue they can easily ruin a book.

To help control these pests, spray with a household insecticide. And, of course, remove the source of the problem, the damp books, to a dry area.

Silverfish.   These fellows could be mentioned again in the section on Food Eaters but I'll cover them now as their varied appetites include fabrics too.

silverfish

They too demolish books, gleefully eating the cloth cover. They can also do a good job on wallpaper, photographs and starched clothes.

For control and prevention:

1. Spray with a substance containing chlordane, diedrin or heptachlor, especially around water pipes and places where dampness accumulates.

2. Try to control the dampness where clothing and books are stored. Investigate some of the products which absorb dampness.

FOOD-EATING INSECTS

Ants. These stubborn nuisances can almost sniff their way from the garden to the gumdrop under the stove. Be sure to wipe up sticky, sweet food spills and sweep away crumbs. Be especially meticulous during the summer months when you have a lot of traffic from outdoors and ice cream, soda and lemonade in the house.

ant

Ant traps are somewhat effective but a liquid spray insecticide containing lindane, diazonon or malathion usually works quite well. Look for the place where the ants are entering the house and if possible seal up the crack. If this is impossible, spray that area liberally and often.

If you have ants in the cabinets or closets, the only way to be rid of them is the hard way. Empty the shelves. Carefully examine all boxes of cereal, sugar and flour and throw out anything that's infested. Spray shelves and leave them empty and airing for one or two hours before replacing their contents. Put all food in tightly covered tins for future prevention.

Cockroaches.   These creatures have been around so long that they even plagued the Egyptian kings in their palaces. Cockroaches are among the few creatures which have survived in their present form from days of antiquity.

They are from about ½ inch to 2 inches in length and vary in color from lightish brown to black.

They love dark, warm, moist places so they are usually found in the kitchen near food sources or in the bathroom. Cockroaches can often be carried in from outside. They love to nestle in the cardboard core of the wrapped

cockroach

toilet paper or in the folded crack of a paper bag. So after the next trip to the market, shake out all things in which they might be hiding.

Cleanliness is important in combating cockroaches but if your neighbor has them, no matter how fastidious you are, chances are you'll have them too. About the only thing you can do then is spray and cope. If the situation is beyond your control, call an exterminator. But if you have only an occasional one buy a surface spray recommended by your hardware dealer.

House flies. These nasty fellows are very able disease carriers so control them before they control you. Their favorite diet is decaying vegetable and animal matter, and

fly

they carry food-poisoning organisms to human food. Flies breed very rapidly and therefore can become very numerous in a short span of time.

To help control this health hazard, be sure garbage-can lids are tight and wash out the cans periodically. Take the garbage out and away from the kitchen at least once or twice each day. Wash out the kitchen waste pail often.

These basic preventive measures will help discourage most pests.

Store food carefully in lidded containers or well-sealed boxes.

Screen your windows in summer and use a space spray (one which is sprayed in the air) to kill them indoors.

Bedbugs.   I'm calling these fellows food eaters. They eat meat—and the meat they eat is you. The reason they're called bedbugs is that they lay their eggs in the tufted portions of mattresses. When hatched, the new bugs naturally make your bed their home.

bedbug

Take the infested mattresses outdoors if possible and spray—but don't soak—them with a surface spray containing pyrethrum. Follow the directions on the can. Wash blankets and bedding and spray cracks and crevices throughout the bedroom.

Mosquitoes.   These pesky fellows are found throughout the warmer months of spring, summer and fall. Their

mosquito

usual breeding place is the stagnant water of a long-standing rain puddle or a sluggish pond. They can also breed in the damp, mulchy leaves which collect in gutters and drainspouts. Be sure gutters and leaders are clean and outdoor drains are free. Work in your community to get rid of sluggish ponds which breed mosquitoes. Screen your windows and use an area spray within the house.

Fleas. These pests can drive your dog or cat into a scratching frenzy. Try not to let your pet roam freely through grasses and brush, as this is where he can pick up fleas. He can also inherit them from other animals. Fleas

flea

are wingless insects only ⅛ inch long but are able to take leaps well in excess of what you might expect. They can easily leap from a fallen bird's nest to the warm comfort of your cocker spaniel's back.

There are many relief treatments available. Inquire at the local pet shop.

Spiders. One of the very few truly poisonous varieties in this country is the black widow. These spiders are

black widow spider

**Note hourglass shape
on underside.**

about ½ inch long, have globelike bodies and are black in color. If you suspect one has bitten you, see your doctor. Other varieties of spiders can give nasty, swelling, itchy bites to those who are susceptible.

To avoid spiders, do not let trash or junk accumulate in the yard. Knock down any webs you see and use an area spray containing chlordane or lindane.

Please, please use your head when handling aerosol sprays. *Do not* spray on dishes or food. Keep your pets away from sprayed areas and remove their food and water bowls. Keep children away from cans and newly sprayed areas.

Do not spray near an open flame or pilot light.

Do not breathe in great amounts of spray. It is toxic.

Do not throw the used can into an incinerator. It is pressurized and will expand and perhaps explode under extreme heat.

RODENTS

Mice.   There are basically two types of mice: domestic house mice and field mice, which come into the house in fall and winter and are, as you might expect, more prevalent in the country. Mice are usually about 3 inches long, excluding the tail. They are not rats but belong to

mouse

the same family. The major physical difference is that mice are smaller and have less scaly tails.

Sure signs that you have mice are their small, dark, seedlike droppings and their gnawing teeth marks. You can easily see these signs in a summer house which has been closed up for a few months. If no food is available they will often go after a bar of soap for its fat content. Mice are not disease carriers but are dangerous because they can gnaw through your electric wiring and perhaps cause a fire.

If possible, get rid of them by using poisoned bait in traps set throughout the house. Mice much prefer chocolate to the well-publicized, traditional cheese. *But do not use poison if you have children or pets.* They often like chocolate too. And try to place the traps where they cannot reach them to minimize the chances of your inquisitive baby or pet getting nipped.

Rats. Common brown rats, sometimes called Norway, wharf or house rats, usually grow to be about 18 inches long, including their scaly, hairless tails. They can swim, burrow, climb and even carry things in their almost manlike hands. They are shrewd, vicious and are seldom seen by day.

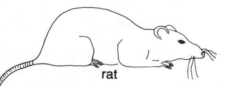

rat

Rats are disease carriers, so get rid of them. Report them to your local authorities as they can cause serious diseases and epidemics. Call a professional exterminator or, if you have a problem with a stray rat roaming around, use poisoned bait just as you would for mice. Place the traps in more concentrated areas, as rats have regular runs and patterns. Follow the directions exactly for using the poison. Remember, this is a poison so be extremely careful when using it around children or pets.

Label the poison can clearly and store it out of the reach of children and unthinking adults. Wash your hands after using the poison.

TERMITES AND ROT

Termites.   Termites are dependent upon dampness and cannot exist without it. They resemble ants and live and work in similar swarms. Only reproducing adults form wings. In the spring, these adults leave the colony and fly out in an attempt to establish their own colonies. After they have done this they shed their now-unnecessary wings and settle down to a steady gnawing routine.

**termite
(without wings)**

Fortunately they are visible insects and the paths that they leave are evident. Look for the tell-tale evidence of shed wings in piles near your home. This is your first warning that a colony is established nearby. If the conditions are favorable (poor ventilation and excess dampness) the colony will thrive.

Your second danger sign is thin, pencil-like mud tunnels, usually running along your foundation. Termites dislike air and light and will build these tunnels between their food source (your wood floors and beams) and the damp ground to which they must return each day. Break up these tunnels and examine the wood near the end of the tunnel. If you suspect that termites have set up housekeeping and are well established, probe with an ice pick. If you can push the pick into the wood one inch or more, the wood will have to be replaced.

You can try to contend with the termites yourself

but since it is hard, strenuous work and requires a great deal of digging and handling poisons, I strongly advise that you hire a professional exterminator. He will do the job well and will often issue a guarantee against future infiltration.

Dry rot. This is a microscopic, plantlike fungus which is actually not particularly dry. In fact its very existence depends on moisture. If the moisture content of your wood is between 20 and 40 percent, dry rot can appear. This air-borne fungus will settle, grow and multiply, feeding on the cellulose fibers of the wood until the weakened cells can no longer hold the wood together. This enables the wood to absorb more moisture, and the dry rot spreads. At some point the weakened beams will no longer be able to support the structure of the house. Let's hope and assume you will notice the problem before the house tumbles down around you.

You can take preventive measures with wood which you know will be susceptible to dampness and rot— fence rails and posts, bottoms of garage doors or house doors, porch beams, joints and steps, wooden gutters and storm windows, to name a few.

Buy a wood preservative containing pentachlorophenol or zinc naphthenate and apply it to this wood. The most effective way is to dip the wood in the solution. If that is impractical, paint or spray the solution until the wood surfaces are well flooded. Be sure to cover all cracks and crevices. Be careful not to get it on your skin; if you do, wash with warm water and soap right away.

For best results, you should remove any wood that has already rotted. But in some cases you can apply the solution to this wood to stop the rotting. Follow the directions on the container.

But remember! Continual dampness will bring trouble. Try to avoid excessive dampness in your home with good ventilation and, if necessary, invest in a dehumidifier. Outdoors, use a wood preservative liberally as a preventive measure.

13. The Happy House Dweller

When you own your own home there are certain responsibilities you must take. These essentially involve the maintenance of the heating system, the grounds and the exterior of the house. Radiators must be fixed, cracked sidewalks repaired, outdoor steps mended, house trim kept clean and painted, lawns cut, gardens weeded and hedges trimmed. In fact, you'll find that most of your spare time in good weather will be devoted to exterior upkeep. So unless you find this work pleasant and rewarding, stick to your convenient apartment.

EXTERIOR MAINTENANCE

If you live in a cold climate and you have been forced by winter weather to neglect your house, here are some points which you should check in the spring.

Spring Check List

1. Check all doors, windows, shutters and trim. Do they need painting?

2. Check all around the foundation for cracks. Check any stone walls, brick walls or walks. Look up at the chimney and try to spot any damage.

3. Check gutters for damage or clogs.

4. Look up at the roof for damage and loose shingles.

| 5. Check cement sidewalks for damage. | 7. Do spring cleanup and yardwork. |
| 6. Check the driveway blacktop. | 8. Check out all tools: mower, rake, shears, etc. |

Painting.   The paint brush usually becomes a permanent extension of the homeowner's hand. Something always needs touching up—trim, fences, doors, lawn furniture and screens (see Chapters 3 and 10). If painting isn't necessary, a good hosing down and scrubbing probably is.

Masonry walls and foundations.   Winter frost has a nasty habit of penetrating masonry, causing cracks.

> 1. Buy ready-mixed cement. There are three varieties. One is used for most repair jobs: cracks, holes and small broken portions; another is for brick work and a third is for building walks, driveways and foundations. Be sure to get the correct one for your repair job. Check with your dealer and ask him to advise you on the amount you'll need. Cement comes in bags from ten to eighty pounds.

> 2. With a cold chisel and hammer, undercut the edges of the crack so that the deepest part of the crack is wider than the surface portion. This will

help insure a good bond between the new cement and the old.

3. Thoroughly clean out any loose chips, dust and dirt. Wet the crack and the area around it with water until the whole area looks damp.

4. Following the proportions printed on the cement bag, mix the cement thoroughly with water. A hoe is an excellent tool with which to do this.

5. Pack the mixed cement into the crack, using a triangular-shaped trowel. Tamp the cement into the crack thoroughly with the point of the trowel, then smooth it flush with the wall surface.

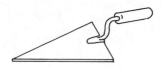

6. Allow the cement to partially harden and then keep the area damp for a couple of days. This will allow the cement to set to its maximum hardness.

Gutters and downspouts.   If you are in a one-story house and you can climb up on a ladder with confidence, get up there in the spring and clean out the gutters. (Second-story ladies on extension ladders deserve a special medal. It's not my way of having fun.) When you climb up to clean, bring the hose up the ladder with you and flush out the downspouts. If debris is too thoroughly packed in the downspout, you may have to use a wire plumber's snake along with the hose to dislodge the gunk.

If you have wooden gutters, give as many surfaces as possible a soaking coat of wood preservative or a clean coat of outdoor paint. Do this only when the wood is dry.

Roof.   If you can climb up on a ladder for a look at your roof, see that none of the shingles look pulled up or are missing. Check the flashing around the chimney and downspouts (this is the metal sheeting which is nailed around these bases).

If you can't get up there, at least go up into the attic and check the attic ceiling for any signs of leakage. Check the ceilings and walls throughout the house for telltale signs of discoloration which might indicate a leak from bad weather. Call a roofer if you suspect problems.

Sidewalks.   Winter weather can batter your sidewalks and driveway. If the concrete has heaved badly, don't attempt to repair it yourself. Call a professional. But if the concrete has small cracks or chips, you can repair it by following the same steps as for repairing masonry. *Be sure to buy the proper premix of cement.*

Blacktop driveway.   If a patch is necessary on a black-top driveway, you can use a prepared asphalt patching compound.

1. Clean out all loose material from the hole.

2. Fill the hole with patching compound to about 1 inch from the surface. Tamp the compound down firmly into the hole, using a log or stout piece of lumber.

3. Add more compound until the surface of the patch is slightly higher than the driveway surface. Tamp this down until it is packed to the level of the surface.

4. After all the holes have been filled, apply a blacktop sealer. This will protect your driveway from oil and grease stains and normal wear and tear. Choose a mild, dry day to do the job. Here's how to use most sealers. (Check the directions on the sealer you buy; directions vary with manufacturers.)

A. Sweep the driveway clean and scrub all stains with water and detergent.

B. Sprinkle the driveway with your hose until it is uniformly wet.

C. Pour the mixed blacktop sealer onto the black-top and spread it evenly over the whole driveway, using a stiff push broom. Allow it to dry for twenty-four hours before using the driveway.

Caulking gun. In the fall, one of your most effective defenses against the coming winter is the caulking gun. Use it to seal up joints and cracks which appear at corners, in stucco and siding, between porch or stoop and house, where window frames meet house siding, or anywhere else a crack could appear.

You can buy caulking in tubes or in a cartridge to use with a caulking gun. Though it costs a little more, I would advise you to buy the disposable gun and cartridge. This eliminates the need to thoroughly clean the gun after each use. Since you will probably not be using the gun very often, it is worth the extra cost to throw it away when the cartridge is empty.

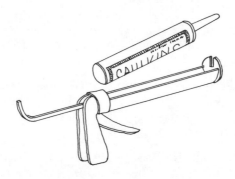

The compound itself is a puttylike substance which usually comes in white, gray or black.

The caulking will not adhere to a dirty or greasy surface. Be sure to clean out the crack with a stiff brush or scrub the surface with detergent and water. It is also advisable to clean out any old caulking before applying new.

Big cracks can be stuffed or packed with oakum or a

similar substitute before you apply the caulking. Inquire at the hardware store.

Apply the caulking according to the directions included with the gun. Squeeze out the caulking, moving the gun at a slow, steady pace and exerting an even pressure on the trigger. The caulking will come out like toothpaste. *Do not* smooth this bead down with your finger or a tool. The caulking is more elastic if left in its toothpastelike ribbon.

STORM WINDOWS AND SCREENS

If it is at all within your budget, the aluminum combination storm windows and screens are absolutely wonderful! No more hoisting and heaving and no more big washing jobs.

A very practical arrangement with these permanent windows is the type which has an upper glass storm window and a lower glass storm window outside with a lower screen inside. In the summer, the lower storm window is pushed up for the season, leaving the screen by itself outside the regular window. The disadvantage of this system is that in the summer you will not have a screen top *and* bottom. I feel that the advantages outweigh this disadvantage. Check with dealers for the style which suits you.

If you're stuck with the old wood-frame storm windows, at least try to hire a husky neighborhood boy to give you a hand. Don't forget to strike your deal with him before he starts as these boys often talk a deal with union wages in mind. Try to find an unworldly fellow. Naturally you'll pay more if he does the washing, so you might want to do this chore yourself.

If you plan to do the whole job, let me warn you, they're heavy. If a wind is blowing be careful. The storm window could pull you right off your feet.

Usually storm windows have a buttonhole-type affair mounted near each corner on top of the frame. This

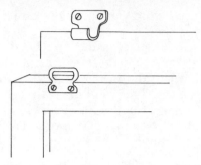

piece of hardware fits into a hook which is mounted on the window frame of the house. The lower portion is often held with a hook and eye.

For a storm window to insulate properly, it should fit into the window frame snugly but not tightly. If it fits loosely and you can feel air coming in around the edges, you can nail a flat weather stripping around the inside edge of the sash. When the storm window is closed the strip presses between the sash and frame. (See Chapter 7 for more information on weather stripping and screening repair.)

If the glass is loose in the storm sash it usually means that the putty has dried out and is no longer effective. This is a delicate job. Using a paring knife and putty knife, chip and scrape away all old putty. Remove the glass and coat the groove where the glass sits with paint. When this has dried, spread putty evenly over the groove. Press the glass on top of this. Insert glazier's points about 4 inches apart around the edges. Then place putty on the outer edge of the frame. (For a more detailed explanation see the section A Broken Window in a Window Frame in Chapter 7.)

YARD WORK

If you want your mower, hose, rake and hoe to be devotedly serviceable, it is a good idea to insure their services by being good to them.

Lawn mower.   If you have a gasoline power mower, take it to be serviced once a year. Your dealer will sharpen the blades, clean and refill the crankcase, clean the old oil from the filter and fill it with fresh oil and clean the sparkplug. Follow his directions to maintain the mower through the summer. Remove grass, leaves and dirt after each use.

If you have a push and puff hand mower do *not* try to sharpen the blades yourself. Clean out all old dirt and dried glass. Oil all moving parts with machine oil. If some sharpening must be done, smear the blades and the strike bar (the plate over which the blades pass when rotating) with the valve-grinding compound used in autos. This will sharpen the blades somewhat. Otherwise have the blades sharpened professionally.

Clippers for edging, pruning, hedges, etc.   Oil all moving parts with machine oil. If you plan to do any sharpening, look carefully at the shape of the bevel on the blade. Follow this bevel when sharpening.

Handtools such as shovels, spades, hoes and rakes. You can buy replacement handles at hardware or garden supply stores, though the replacement may seem complicated. Take the tool with you to make sure you buy a properly matched replacement. Your dealer, if he is a kindly man, will explain how that particular handle fits on your tool.

With a wire brush, scrub the face and back of a shovel, hoe or rake to remove caked-on dirt and corrosion. Then rub down the metal with a rag dipped in penetrating oil. Clean all wood handles thoroughly and apply a coating of linseed oil or marine varnish.

In the fall, clean all gardening tools and rub a thin coat of oil over them to prevent rust. Store in a dry place until spring.

Garden hose and nozzle.   Replace all the rubber washers in all fittings so that they will be snug without leaks.

If your rubber hose has developed a small leak, coat the area with a thick coating of black rubber-base cement. Let this dry and then apply a second, thin coat and wrap a single layer of plastic friction tape around the hose. Hold the tape firmly in your hand for a minute or so until the cement dries.

Here's how to repair a large leak:

1. Cut off the defective area with a sharp knife as squarely as possible.

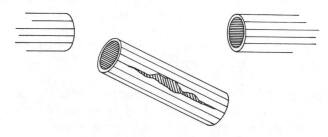

2. Bring the broken piece to the hardware store to use as a size sample. Ask for a coupling splicer which will fit the broken piece.

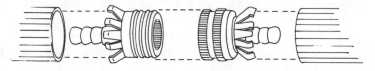

3. Insert one end of the coupling flush into one piece of hose. Tap the fingers or prongs of the coupling gently and gradually until all prongs grip the hose tightly.

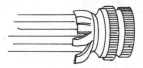

4. Insert the other end of the coupling into the other piece of hose and tap the prongs snugly. Then screw the two pieces together.

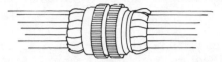

You can use this type of hose coupling for both rubber and plastic hoses.

There are other types of fittings which are used specifically for plastic hoses. They are forced into the ends of the hose instead of being clamped on top. Here's how to use one style.

1. Dip one end of the plastic hose into hot water to soften it so that you can insert the flanged tube into the hose end with ease.

2. Slip the flanged tube into the hose.

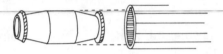

3. Slip the larger end of the threaded coupling over the flanged tube and tighten the coupling with a screwing motion onto the hose.

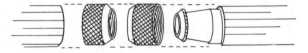

4. Then slide the smaller end of the second coupling over the other end of the flanged tube. Push the flanged tube into the other piece of hose, following the directions in Step 1.

5. Screw the second coupling tightly onto the hose.

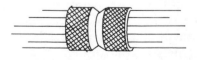

Here's how to store your hose in the fall.

1. Drain all water from it.

2. Remove all nozzles and washers. Clean them and store them in a container or jar.

3. Make sure all kinks are out of the hose.

4. When the hose is thoroughly dry, coil it and store it on a hose reel.

Outdoor water taps.   Before freezing weather comes, turn off outdoor water taps to avoid freezing pipes. After turning off the tap source, be sure to turn on the tap handle so all the water will drain out. Leave the tap open until spring.

HEATING

Here are a few helpful hints to help you maintain your heating system.

1. Once the thermostat is set, it's up to the furnace to turn itself off and on, according to the temperature dictated by the thermostat. Here are a few tips for your comfort and economy.

A. Don't be a thermostat wriggler. Put the dial at a comfortable setting for you and your family and leave it that way. Most people are happy between 72 and 75 degrees in the daytime. You may choose to lower the temperature at night to somewhere between 66 to 70 degrees.

B. The thermostat is highly sensitive to the air around it. If you play a radio or light a lamp near it, it will think the room is nice and warm and will dutifully cease performing. Meanwhile you may be sitting in your own cold breath. Avoid using anything that generates heat (or cold) near the thermostat control.

2. If your basement or house is extremely damp, especially in summer, consider investing in a dehumidifier. This unit, measuring approximately 2 feet by 3 feet, can be hooked up with a hose over a basement drain.

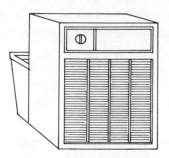

Alternatively, you can empty the water container by hand every three days or so to avoid overflowing. This investment will end destruction from mold and mildew.

3. If someone in the house suffers greatly from a dust allergy, you can install an electronic air-cleaning system. This unit eliminates about 90 percent of the airborne dust and almost 100 percent of the pollen that passes through the system. Inquire about this at a heating supply dealer.

4. You can substantially reduce heat loss with insulation and properly fitted doors and windows. If your house is not insulated, seriously consider having at least the attic done. You'll be more comfortable in both winter and summer and the saving in fuel costs will quickly pay for the cost of the insulating.

A surprising amount of heat can also escape through ill-fitting doors and windows. See Chapter 7 for instructions on fixing doors and windows and installing weather stripping.

5. Your heating system should be inspected at least once during the year. Leave all major adjustments and repairs to the heating serviceman. However,

there are a few things you can do to keep things ticking smoothly.

A. Remove dust and lint from all radiator grills and openings and from in between the fins (heating plates). Don't let drapes, carpets or pieces of furniture interfere with the heat flow.

B. In steam- heated homes faulty radiator escape valves are a common cause of uneven heating. These valves allow built-up air to escape automatically. If this air cannot escape there will be no room for the steam. Hence, cold radiators. Here's how to replace the valve.

1. Turn off the main heat valve at the radiator base.

2. Unscrew the escape valve, take it to the hardware store and buy a new one to match.

3. Screw the new escape valve on.

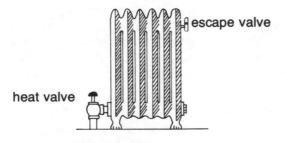

Some of the more modern radiators have a fancy shell over the basic heating unit. Look for little special doors and compartments in this shell which open to reveal the necessary valves.

C. Some hot-water heating systems have a small key fitting on each radiator. Two or three times during the winter turn the key (which looks like a child's skate key) counterclockwise to bleed off excess air in the radiator. Hold a bowl under this valve to catch the small amount of water which appears when the last air is released. As soon as the water appears, close the valve by turning the key clockwise. A few systems have a screw that works in the same manner as the key.

It is best to drain these radiators by starting on the top floor and working your way down.

Be sure the room where your furnace or boiler is situated has good ventilation. The burner can become oxygen starved, and poisonous gases could be released through the house.

Know where the furnace shut-off is located. If you smell burning fuel and an open window won't air it away, shut off the furnace and call your serviceman immediately.

14. Household Emergencies

FIRE

A fire is one of the most feared disasters that can happen in your home. But you can take certain preventive measures.

1. Be sure your wiring is in good condition and is not constantly overloaded. Know how to turn off the electrical source in your home.

2. Be sure your chimney is clean and in good condition and that there are no leaks or holes in the mortar between stones and brick.

3. Always use a fire screen in front of an open fireplace. The fire without a screen may look very pretty but the results after a conflagration will not.

4. Keep your oven and broiler clean so that last week's grease and fat cannot catch fire. Keep a small fire extinguisher by the oven and use it on any fat fire. These fire fighters are very reasonable in price today and are compact for easy storage. You might

consider buying a few to put throughout the house and in the furnace room.

5. Smokers—use your heads. Never forget when you are smoking. Keep that cigarette foremost in your mind.

6. Be sure your furnace is clean and in good working order.

7. Know all the exits available to you in case of fire. If you live where there are fire escapes, know how to get to them. If your fire escapes aren't being maintained, be sure to let the management know.

8. If you have no fire extinguisher (shame on you) and grease catches fire when you are cooking, do not use water on it. Douse it with salt.

Do not waste much time trying to control a fire. Call the fire department! They would much rather be called out on a fire that you were able to control after all than one to which they were called too late.

FLOODS

A great deal of damage can be done by an overflowing toilet or washing machine or even a faucet which won't turn off. Know how to turn off the particular fixture and how to turn off the water entirely. The most immediate thing to do in the event of a sudden flood is to grab towels and sheets to try to contain the water before you go to the turn-off valve.

GAS LEAKS

If you smell a gas leak and it's not because a pilot light is out, shut off the main gas control quickly and call the gas company.

FIRST AID

Have a first-aid book in your home and become familiar with its contents. I'll mention a few of the most frequent and most dangerous household accidents. But be sure to read more about them in your first-aid book.

Keep emergency numbers handy by your telephone.

Burns (minor).   Immediately run cold tap water over the burn. This treatment will relieve the pain and often prevent blistering. If there is no blistering, use a first-aid or burn salve. If the burned area has blistered, it is very susceptible to infection. Do not break or try to drain the blister and do not put salve on it. Cover the burn with sterile dressings in order to exclude air and prevent contamination. At any sign of infection see a doctor.

If the minor burn covers a large area, go to the doctor. This type of burn can be dangerous.

Burns (major).   Have the victim lie down to avoid shock. *Do not* apply any ointments, oil or antiseptics. Wash your hands thoroughly and cover the burn with sterile dressing or with freshly laundered sheets which are completely dry. This is done to exclude contaminating air as burns are highly susceptible to infection.

Cuts (minor).   Wash your hands thoroughly before treating any wound.

Clean the area around the wound with soap and running tap water. Then wash the wound itself with running water. Clean out all dirt. If necessary use sterile tweezers to remove matter from the wound. (Sterilize them by boiling in water for ten minutes.)

Apply a mild antiseptic to the wound and the surrounding area. Then cover the wound with sterile gauze and one of the new "hurtless" adhesive tapes. If infection occurs see your doctor.

Cuts (major).   With sterile gauze, apply pressure directly over the wound. When the bleeding has stopped, bandage the dressing in place firmly. See your doctor as soon as possible. (See the first-aid book for pressure points when needed.)

Electrical shock. As quickly as possible break the victim's contact with the source of current. *Do not* touch the victim yourself. Either pull out the electric plug or pry the victim away from the current, using a dry pole, rope or tree branch. Be sure you are standing on dry ground.

Once contact has been broken you may touch the victim. Do not move him but be sure he is breathing. If he is not, apply mouth-to-mouth resuscitation. You should know how to do this—see your first aid book.

Call a doctor or ambulance.

STAINS

Do the following as quickly as possible.

Alcoholic beverages. Sponge with cold water.

Ball point. Rub stain gently with petroleum jelly. Then following with cleaning fluid.

Blood. Soak in cold water. If it is a nonwashable fabric, sponge with cool water.

Candle wax. Scrape with dull knife. Place cloth between two blotters and press with warm iron. Follow with cleaning fluid.

Chewing gum. Pick off as much as possible. Sponge with cleaning fluid.

Chocolate. Scrape off excess with a dull knife. Wash in warm, soapy water. Rinse.

Coffee and tea. Soak in cool water. With milk: first use cleaning fluid, then soak in cool water, then wash in warm suds.

Egg. Sponge with cold water. Then use cleaning fluid.

Grass. Soak in warm suds or one of the presoakers. If persistent, sponge with denatured alcohol.

Greasy or oily foods. Sponge with cleaning fluid. Then wash in warm, soapy water.

Ink. Run cool water over the stain. Wash in warm, soapy water with a bit of ammonia added. Rinse.

Lipstick. Rub with cleaning fluid. Wash in warm, soapy water. Rinse.

Mildew. Rub off as much as possible. Wash in warm, soapy water. Rinse.

Paint (latex). Soak up as much as possible. Wash immediately in cool water.

Paint (oil). Soak up as much as possible. Soak in turpentine. Wash.

Perspiration. Sponge area with a diluted solution of vinegar in water. Sponge again in clear water.

Rust. Squeeze lemon juice onto the stain and rub. Before it dries, rinse in warm water.

Scorch. Wash with soapy water and a mild bleach. Rinse. A dark scorch is usually beyond repair.

Shoe polish. Scrape off excess. Rub gently with dry cleaning fluid, turning the rubbing cloth frequently.

Tar. Scrape off as much as possible. Rub stain with petroleum jelly. Then sponge with cleaning fluid. Wash in warm, soapy water. Rinse.

Wine. Pour salt and club soda on still-damp wine stain. This will absorb it. Sponge with cool water.

Glossary

Many of the following terms have various meanings. I use only the one that applies to home repair.

A

Abrasive. Something used to wear away a surface, such as sandpaper on wood.

Across (against) the grain. At a 90-degree angle to the direction of the grain of a piece of wood. Never sand wood against the grain.

Adapter. A hardware item used to adjust a tool so that it may be used in a manner to suit you. Example: a three-hole adapter for plugging in an electric drill (p. 67).

Air space. The space between a wall and its outer structure (see Hollow Wall, Ch. 2) or a floor and base (p. 101).

Anchor bolt. A hardware item that fastens something firmly to a wall, floor or ceiling (Ch. 2).

Angle iron. An L-shaped metal tool used to attach a shelf to a wall (pp. 15–17) or to brace corners on screens (p. 91) or chairs (p. 158).

Ants. Small, social insects that burrow in the ground. Household pests that can be controlled (p. 178).

Asbestos tiles. Floor tiles made from asbestos, a nonflammable material (p. 100).

Asphalt. A road covering made from a variety of the mineral bitumen. Asphalt patching compound is used to repair blacktop driveways (p. 189).

Asphalt tiles. Floor tiles made from asphalt (p. 100).

Auger. A tool similar to a drill bit, for boring holes or clearing pipes (p. 188).

Awl, threaded. A pointed tool for piercing holes; especially useful for making small holes in wood (pp. 9–10).

B

Back saw. Used to cut moldings, miters and accurate joints. Gives a very smooth cut (p. 134).

Baseboard. The board used at the base of a wall as a decorative finishing device (pp. 38, 120).

Battery. An apparatus used to generate electrical power, as in a flashlight (p. 79).

Bedbugs. Household pests that infest mattresses (p. 180).

Bed slats. Boards used in a series to support a box-spring mattress on the frame of the bed (pp. 151–152).

Benzine. A clear, flammable liquid made from petroleum, used as a solvent and cleaning fluid (pp. 171–172).

Bit. A replaceable tool inserted into the end of the brace. This tool does the actual boring of the hole and its size determines the width of the hole (p. 5).

Blacktop. A road or driveway topping (p. 189).

Boiler. A large, metal container in which steam is gathered for use as a power force (p. 199).

Bolt. A metal rod, usually threaded, with a head on one end. The other end often accepts a nut (p. 12).

Book lice. Household pests that destroy books (pp. 176–177).

Brace. A crank-shaped tool commonly referred to as a drill, used with a bit for boring holes (p. 5).

Brad. A short, thin, wirelike nail used for finishing (p. 11).

Buffer. Tool used to polish or shine, as in finishing floors (p. 121). Buff furniture by hand with steel wool (p. 144).

C

Cane. Bamboo or rattan; used in wickerwork (pp. 163–164).

Cap (electrical). Portion of a lamp switch that covers the wires leading into the switch (pp. 75–77).

Carpet beetles. Household pests that eat clothing (p. 176).

Casement window. A window style that swings outward on hinges (pp. 39–40, 86–87).

Casters. A set of small wheels supporting a piece of furniture to give it mobility (p. 155).

Caulking. Soft, puttylike material that plugs seams tightly. Used with caulking gun (pp. 190–191).

Caulking gun. Used to apply caulking or adhesive to secure wood paneling (pp. 127, 132, 135) or ceramic tiles (pp. 137–138) or to seal cracks in the house exterior (pp. 190–191).

C-clamp. A clamp shaped like the letter C, often used for holding together items such as furniture while glue is drying (p. 159).

Cement. Powdered lime and clay mixed with water; used for paving or as a mortar (pp. 187–189).

Ceramic tiles. Potterylike baked tiles used on walls and floors, especially in bathrooms and kitchens (pp. 136–138).

Chair webbing. Strips of strong material used to support cushioning portions of a chair or couch (pp. 161–163).

Chisel. A cutting tool with a beveled edge, used to carve, cut or mortise (p. 117); the act of cutting or mortising.

Chuck. An attachment for holding a tool in a machine. On

a brace, the end into which the bit is inserted (p. 5).
Circuit breaker. A device that breaks a circuit that is not behaving correctly so that it cannot cause damage (pp. 64, 66).
Claw. The forked end of a hammer's head, used to pull out nails (p. 2).
Closet auger. A cranklike apparatus used to clear a clogged toilet bowl (p. 61).
Cockroach. A pest insect infesting residences; can be controlled (pp. 178–179).
Cold chisel. A heavy-duty chisel used for breaking up concrete or any other tough material; used to remove ceramic tiles (pp. 136–138) and for repairing masonry (p. 187).
Common nails. Standard nails of varying sizes with normalsized heads (p. 10).
Concrete. Sand, gravel, cement and water mixed together to form a paving or mortar; used for walls (pp. 14–15, 187), floors (pp. 101–102, 104) and sidewalks (p. 189).
Coping saw. A very thin, ribbonlike saw blade stretched onto a U-shaped frame; used to cut curves and fancy shapes in thin wood or plastic (p. 4).
Cork panels. Paneling or wall covering made of cork (pp. 125, 135).
Countersink. To sink a nail below the surface of wood (p. 2).
Coupling. A connecting unit that fastens one item to another, as in repairing a garden hose (194–195).
Crosscut saw. A saw with teeth arranged especially to cut comfortably across the grain of wood (p. 3).

D
Dehumidifier. An electrical appliance that removes moisture from the air; useful in controlling mildew and dry rot (pp. 185, 197).
Disk sander. A small floor-sanding machine with sandpaper on a disk that spins, used for edges (pp. 119–120).
Double-hung window. A window that slides up or down on a track with a pulley and weight arrangement (pp. 39–40, 81–85).
Dowel. A peg used to fasten two pieces of wood together, as in a bedpost (pp. 153–154).
Downspout. A pipe attached to a gutter to draw off rainwater from a roof (p. 188).
Drill. A tool with a sharp edge, used for boring holes (p. 5).
Drop cloth. A large cloth thrown down to protect floors or furniture when you are painting (pp. 32–33).
Drum sander. A heavy-duty sanding machine (pp. 119–120).
Dry rot. Fungus that can destroy damp wood (p. 185).
Dry wall. Wall made of plasterboard, fiberboard, wood panels or any other dry material, i.e., not plaster (p. 135).

E

Elbow joint. A curved pipe used to join one straight pipe to another, forming an angle; used in sinks (p. 51).

Elbow plug. A removable plug used to drain an elbow joint (p. 51); it may leak and need repairing (p. 52).

Emery paper. An abrasive paper used to smooth wood or metal, similar to fine sandpaper (p. 86).

Enamel. A hard-surfaced, glossy-finished paint (end sheet); use for cabinets (pp. 40–41), floors (p. 122) and furniture (pp. 146–147, 149–150, 155).

Escape valve. A valve, as on a radiator, that is activated when too much energy builds up. The excess energy (steam) escapes through the valve (p. 198).

F

Faucet washer. A ring of rubber or plastic used to help control the flow of water (pp. 53–54).

Fiber glass. Material made of finely spun fibers of glass, used in screening (pp. 88, 91).

Finial. A decorative ornament at the top of a lamp or bedpost (pp. 152, 153–154).

Finishing nail. A nail with a small head; can be countersunk below the surface of a piece of wood (p. 11).

Flashing. A waterproof sheathing often used around chimney bases (p. 189).

Fleas. Pests that infect dogs and cats (p. 181).

Float ball and arm. Part of the mechanism in a toilet tank that helps the toilet to flush (pp. 58–60).

Float valve. Same as above.

Flush. Directly butting or snug up against another item.

Fluorescent light. An illumination caused by activating phosphorescent materials (pp. 77–79).

Force cup. Often called plumber's helper. Used to suction out a clogged drain (p. 51) or toilet (p. 61).

Friction tape. Similar to electrician's tape; also used to mend garden hoses (p. 194).

Furring strips. Narrow strips of wood from a fir tree, used to prepare walls for wood paneling (p. 127, 128–129).

Fuse. A device that breaks a circuit that is not behaving properly so it cannot cause damage (pp. 64–65).

G

Glazier's points. Small metal fastenings set into the wooden frame of a windowpane to support the pane (pp. 83–84, 192). For metal windows, substitute glazing clips (p. 87).

Glazing compound. A pastelike putty used on the edges of windowpanes and frames; there are different types for wood or metal frames (pp. 85, 86, 87, 192).

Globe faucet. Common style of faucet (pp. 53–55).

Grain (wood). The direction of the texture of the wood. Always sand wood with the grain, as in floors (p. 120) or furniture (p. 142).

Graphite powder. Used as a lubricant where a liquid lubricant is not recommended, as in door locks (p. 98).

Ground (electrical). The connection between an electrical circuit and the earth; grounding wire (pp. 67–74).

Gutter. A trough at the roof edge to catch rainwater (p. 188).

H

Hacksaw. A narrow-bladed saw used for cutting metal (p. 4).

Half round. A strip of wood cut in the shape of a semicircle, used as a molding.

Hardware. Items such as machine parts, tools, fittings and utensils, all made of metal.

Hinge. A piece of hardware that swings on a pivot. Most commonly used on box lids or on doors (p. 93).

Hollow wall. A wall, usually inside, with air space behind. Very often a dry wall (pp. 14–19, 128).

Hot air heat. Heat produced throughout a building using forced hot air and hot air ducts.

Hot water heat. Heat produced by hot water circulating through pipes to radiators (pp. 198–199).

House flies. Disease-carrying household pests (pp. 179–180).

I

Incandescent light. A source of illumination that heats a filament in a vacuum until it glows (p. 77).

Insecticide. Chemicals combined to control insects.

Insulation (home). A material used on house walls and roofs to keep heat in in winter and out in summer (p. 197).

J

Jacknut. A small piece of hardware used as an anchor, as on a hollow door or wood paneling (p. 20).

Joint. A point where two items join. Example: a pipe elbow.

K

Keyhole saw. A narrow, tapered saw blade for making curved cuts and widening and shaping holes (p. 103).

L

Lacquer. A clear finish made of shellac gum resins dissolved in alcohol, usually used as a finish for wood.

Latex. A water emulsion of synthetic rubber or plastic, used in the manufacture of certain paints (p. 204); use these water-soluble latex paints for walls and ceiling (p. 33) and for some floors (p. 122).

Lath. Thin strips of wood attached to a building frame as a base for plaster (often called furring strips)

Level, carpenter's. A tool used to measure the horizontal or vertical level of an item, used in wood paneling (p. 127).

Lift rod. Part of the mechanism of a toilet tank that controls the flow of water into the bowl (p. 57).

M

Machine oil. Clear oil used to lubricate machiney (p. 80).

Mason. A man who works in cement, brick and stone.

Masonry. Something built by a mason (pp. 15–16, 187–188).

Masonry bit. A tool with which to bore through masonry or brick. Often referred to as a "star" drill (p. 16).

Mastic. Resin obtained from a Mediterranean evergreen tree, used as a varnish or cement, as on a concrete floor before tile is laid (p. 101).

Mending plate. A plate, usually of metal, with screw holes; it is screwed into an item such as a chair for added strength (p. 160).

Mice. Small rodents; household pests that can be controlled (pp. 182–183).

Miter. To cut two sections of a joint to form a corner.

Miter box. A box used as a guide into which wood to be mitered is fit (pp. 134, 152, 158, 168).

Molding. A shaped strip of wood often used decoratively at the base or top of a room (pp. 104, 127–128, 132–135).

Molly bolt. An anchor that holds an item securely on a hollow wall (pp. 17–19).

Mosquitoes. Summer pests that can be controlled (pp. 180–181).

Moths. Household pests that cat clothing (pp. 175–176).

N

Nailset. A tool used to countersink a nail (p. 118).

Nut. A small block, usually metal, with a threaded hole in its center that screws onto a bolt (p. 12).

O

Oakum. A caulking used mostly in the seams of boats or in cracks in masonry (p. 190).

Orbital sander. A sanding machine that revolves in an orbital motion.

Overflow. A safety drain in a sink or tub in case the water level rises too high (p. 50).

P

Packing. Stringlike substance packed into a portion of a faucet to help control the flow of water (p. 55).

Packing nut. Part of the workings of a faucet (p. 54).

Paraffin. A waxy substance made from petroleum; used to lubricate balky windows (p. 82) or drawers (p. 166).

Penetrating oil. An oil refined for deep penetration into rust, used on steel windows (p. 86) and garden tools (p. 193).

Pilot hole. A small hole, usually made by a threaded awl, to be used as a guide for a screw or drilled hole (p. 9).

Plaster. A mixture of lime, sand and water often used on interior walls. Plaster walls are known as wet walls.

Plasterboard. A dry wall of plaster-coated, lightweight fiberboard (p. 135).

Plaster, patching. Powder that is mixed with water; used to fill large cracks and holes in walls (pp. 32, 35).

Pliers. A pincer or nutcrackerlike tool for holding tightly to small items (p. 8).

Plug. A drain to draw off water from a pipe (p. 51).

Plumb line. A lead weight hung on the end of a line; used to determine the vertical of a wall. Used in applying wallpaper (pp. 43, 45) and paneling (pp. 127, 130–131).

Plumber's helper. See Force Cup.

Plumber's snake. A thin, flexible cable used to clean out drains (pp. 51–52) and downspouts (p. 188).

Plywood. A sheet of construction material made of thin layers of wood pressed together and glued; its uses include door panels (p. 19), underflooring for tiles (pp. 102–103) and wall paneling (Ch. 9).

Primer. An undercoat or first coat of paint used to prepare a surface to receive the final paint (p. 31).

Pry bar. A metal bar used as a prying lever; used to remove moldings (p. 127).

Pulley. A grooved wheel into which a rope is threaded, used to raise and lower weights, such as a window (p. 83).

Putty. A pliable substance of chalk and linseed oil, used to fill cracks and secure window panes (p. 84, 85–86, 192).

Q

Quarter round. Molding for corners; also known as shoe molding (p. 133).

R

Rabbet. A groove cut at the edge of a piece of wood, as in a drawer (p. 167).

Rats. Disease-carrying rodents (p. 183–184).

Rattan. A climbing palm tree whose tough, thin stems are used in wickerwork (p. 150, 164–165).

Red lead. Paint used as a rust retardant on metal windows (pp. 86–87) and other metal surfaces.

Ringed nails. Used in flooring (p. 102).

Ripsaw. A saw whose teeth are arranged especially to cut comfortably along the length (with the grain) of a piece of wood.

Rottenstone. A substance derived from decomposed limestone, used for polishing and removing stains from wood surfaces (p. 171).

Routed. Grooved out, as in wood (p. 167).

S

Sabre saw. A handheld power saw with a slender blade, useful in cutting wood paneling (p. 126).

Sandpaper. A paper coated on one side with abrasive sand; used for smoothing or polishing.

Sash. A frame for holding window glass.

Sash brush. A paintbrush especially shaped to get into the corners of window sashes (p. 39).

Sash chain. Used in combination with pulley sash weights for ease in opening and closing windows (p. 83).

Sash cord. Predecessor to sash chain. Rarely used now (p. 83).

Sash weight. Used in combination with pulley and sash chain for ease in opening and closing windows.

Saw. A cutting tool made of a thin, metal blade with sharp, jagged, ripping teeth (pp. 3–4).

Screwdriver. A tool to drive and remove screws (pp. 6–7).

Screw eyes. A screw that instead of having a head, ends in a closed loop. Used on picture frames (pp. 13, 24–25).

Sealer. A coat of paint or other finish used to seal the open pores of new wood or plaster; used in painting walls (pp. 35, 204) and finishing floors (p. 121) and furniture (pp. 142, 148, 149).

Seam roller. A tool used to flatten out the seams of newly glued wallpaper (pp. 42–47).

Shell (electrical). The covered part of a lamp switch (pp. 75–77).

Shellac. A flaky resin; combined with alcohol, used as a wood filler or finish on floors (p. 121) and furniture (pp. 144, 146, 166).

Shim. Paper or cardboard inserted behind a hinge to correct an imbalance, as in a door (pp. 94, 96) or behind furring strips (p. 129).

Shingles. Thin wedges of wood, slate or composition material used in overlapping fashion to cover a roof (p. 189).

Silicone lubricant. Used to lubricate balky drawers (p. 166).

Sill. See Stop Molding.

Silverfish. Household pests that thrive on dampness (p. 177).

Solid wall. A wall of brick or concrete, usually an outside wall (pp. 14–17).

Solvent. A thinner or dissolver.

Spackle. A premixed, plasterlike compound for filling small cracks and holes in a wall (pp. 32, 34–35).

Spiders. Insects that give nasty bites (pp. 181–182).

Spiral nails. Used in flooring (pp. 102, 118–120).

Square, carpenter's. A perfect 90-degree angle, used to check measurements, as in laying tiles (pp. 104, 105, 116).

Stain. A dye for staining wood (pp. 141–143, 170).

Staple gun. A tool used to eject staples with force (p. 10);

useful in repairing furniture (pp. 156, 161–162).

Steam heat. A mixture of hot air and hot vapor that rises in pipes to heat a building (p. 198).

Stem washer. A washer of plastic or rubber used in the stem of a faucet to help control the flow of water (p. 54).

Stop molding. Molding used at the base of a window or doorway; also called a sill (pp. 81, 82–83).

Stopper ball. A mechanism in the tank of a toilet that stops the flow of water into the bowl (pp. 57–58).

Striker plate. The plate on the door frame into which the door latch fits (pp. 95–96).

Studs. Wall timbers that are part of the main structure of a building. You must attach heavy wall units and furring strips to the studs (pp. 28, 128).

Suspended floor. A floor with air space underneath (p. 101).

T

Tank ball. See Stopper Ball.

Terminal. Each end of an electrical circuit.

Terminal screw. The screw around which a terminal is wound, as in plugs (pp. 67–68) and lamps (pp. 75–76).

Termites. Wood-boring insects (pp. 184–185).

Thermostat. A mechanism that automatically controls a heating element or unit (p. 196).

T-nut. Small piece of hardware used as an anchor on a single thickness of wood such as a panel door (pp. 22–23).

Tongue and groove. Boards, usually used in flooring, that are cut and ridged so that one board's notch fits into the next board's groove (pp. 116–118).

Trap. A portion of a drainpipe that captures debris (p. 51).

Trowel. A flat tool with a handle, used for applying cement or smoothing plaster (pp. 101, 188).

Turnoff valve. A valve used to shut off the flow of steam, fuel, water, etc. through a pipe (p. 48).

U

Undercut. To cut out a crack in a wall so that the inner portion of the crack is wider than the surface portion. This insures a secure bond for patching material (p. 34).

Underwriter's knot. Knot used to fasten wires in a plug (pp. 69–70).

V

Valve seat. Ridge inside a faucet on which the valve stem rests (p. 55).

Valve stem (spindle). Part of a faucet; helps to control the flow of water (p. 54).

Varnish. Resins in linseed oil, alcohol, etc., used to give a shiny, glossy finish to floors (p. 121) and furniture (pp. 143–144, 166, 170).

Veneer. A thin sheet of fine-quality wood, used to cover other wood (pp. 172–174).

Vinyl cove base. Vinyl molded like wood cove molding, used as a finishing device at the base of a wall (p. 111).

Vinyl tiles. Durable flooring tiles (pp. 100, 103–113, 124).

W

Wall size. A glue that prepares walls for wallpaper (p. 44).

Washer. A doughnut-shaped ring of metal, rubber, cork, leather or plastic that cushions a bolt to fit tightly. Used in faucets (pp. 49, 53–54) and hoses (p. 193).

Wax. A pliable substance used as a protective polish for aluminum windows (p. 87), for floors (pp. 123–124) and furniture (p. 143, 149, 171, 172).

Weather stripping. Strips of material, made of felt, rubber, fiber glass or metal, used around windows or doors as insulation (p. 96–97).

Web clamp. A clamp made of webbing, often used to hold together furniture being glued (p. 170).

Wedge. A triangular-shaped tool used to split wood or to force something apart; used in furniture repair (p. 158).

Wet wall. Wall made of plaster.

Wicker. See Rattan.

Widows. Dribbles of paint that dry as bumps.

Wood panels. Manufactured panels of standard size (often 4 by 8 feet), used to cover walls (pp. 125–135).

Wrench. A tool for screwing nuts, bolts, pipes, etc. (pp. 8–9); especially useful in plumbing repairs (Ch. 5).

CHOOSING THE RIGHT PAINT

Paint	Its use	Reason to use
ENAMEL (indoor, outdoor) A high-gloss paint	Kitchen, bathroom, on walls. Wood trim. Wood or steel windows. Windowsills. Furniture, bookcases, doors.	Very durable. Easily maintained. Can be washed and scrubbed with little concern for surface damage.
SEMIGLOSS (oil or latex base) slightly shiny	Kitchen, bathroom, on walls. Wood trim. Wood window frames. Windowsills. Furniture. Bookcases, doors.	If you object to the very high gloss of enamel, this is almost as easy to maintain and can be washed successfully.
FLAT (oil or latex base) An absolutely matte finish	Plaster walls and ceilings. Dry walls. Wood paneling. Room trim and doors.	Flat, even color is desirable on wall areas. It can be used on trim but is not particularly washable.
PRIMER AND SEALER for wood or walls	On raw wood or newly plastered walls. To cover a dark color before applying light-colored paint.	Use before painting to seal the pores of the wood so that the paint will not soak into the wood. Use also to prime or prepare the surface to accept the paint.